turning points

life's twists and turns

with a foreword by Patricia Charpentier

Cover and interior design by Joan Keyes,
Dovetail Publishing Services

ISBN-13: 978-1-939472-40-3

Photo of Ollie in "Seven or Seventy-Seven: It's Still Puppy Love"
by Susan D. Owens taken by Carol Gatto

Published by LifeStory Publishing, a division of Writing Your Life
P.O. Box 541527
Orlando, Florida 32854
WritingYourLife.org
First Edition: January 2023
Printed in the USA
10 9 8 7 6 5 4 3 2

Dedication

To the authors of these amazing stories, all the members of Life Writers, and those everywhere who long to share their memories in writing.

Thank you for your wisdom and sharing it with us.

Patricia & Life Writers

Acknowledgments

No book is ever published without the touch of many hands, so it is with this first Life Writers anthology.

Thank you to all the authors who wrote, edited, and revised their stories multiple times. Your willingness to lay your heart out on the page and allow us into your world touches and inspires me.

Many thanks to Writing Your Life editor extraordinaire Teresa TL Bruce for her suggestions and for making good stories even better.

Thank you to Life Writer Etya Krichmar for proofreading the final manuscript.

Thank you, Life Writer Lou Martindale, for readying our photos for publication.

Thank you to Joan Keyes of Dovetail Publishing Services for her keen eye and sense of style. You dressed us up in our Sunday best.

And a huge thank you to Millie Ford for the thorough job she did in managing this project. Without you and your dedicated efforts, this book would not have materialized.

Contents

Foreword

In March 2020, our world became much smaller, and we added new words to our vocabulary: coronavirus, SARS-CoV, and COVID-19, among others. Restaurants and shops closed. People went home to work. Masks were mandatory accessories. Coughs and sneezes filled us with fear. The number of new cases and deaths from this then-little-known virus rose each day.

I looked for some small thing I could do to take individuals' minds off the chaos in our world for just a few minutes and decided to run a free, online seven-day writing challenge. Every day, I sent out a writing prompt designed to trigger memories and asked participants to write a response and then share it with the group. More than 200 people from across the United States, Canada, Australia, New Zealand, Japan, Egypt, and India answered the call and began writing.

At the end of the challenge, a core group of active participants asked, "What are we going to do now?"

I hadn't planned for anything to follow the challenge, so off the top of my head, I said, "I can do a four-week class." Twenty or so people signed up, and we continued to write together for another month.

When the class ended, again, this core group asked, "What are we going to do now?"

I had no intention to continue teaching online classes. Still, I offered another four-week session, and the same people signed up, wrote their stories, read each other's stories, provided supportive and encouraging feedback—and became friends.

By this time, I anticipated the group's request at month's end. It came, and I offered, "Would any of you be interested in an online membership that includes what we've been doing in these classes plus a few extras?"

A resounding yes immediately followed, and the online Life Writers membership launched in October 2020.

More than two years later, Life Writers remains a dynamic, caring, supportive group. We've picked up new writers along the way, but many of that original group still draft new pieces and remain part of our vibrant writing community.

What you hold in your hands is a sampling of the outstanding stories written by twenty-one Life Writers. They include some who never finished high school and others who hold multiple advanced degrees. Their ages range from one in her mid-forties to 105-year-old Lucille Ellson. Many are prolific and write daily; other writers draft stories only when a memory corners them and won't let go. Several have published one or more books. For others, this is the first time to see their names in print. Some authors have been writing since childhood; others never wrote a word until they joined the group. Several Life Writers write in a second language. But all of our authors share a deep belief that their stories are important and should be written from the heart.

The stories on these pages will make you laugh and cry, and you might recall moments you haven't thought about in ages. You can vicariously experience the life of a frazzled farm wife, the horror of losing one's sight, the unique talent of impersonating classic cars, the joy of becoming a grandmother amid profound grief, the love between a mother and her children, the blessing of teaching blind students to read and write Braille, the dance of a lifetime under the stars while at sea, and much, much more.

To say I am proud of these and all our Life Writers is a gross understatement. Writing life stories isn't effortless, but the rewards are great, as each of these authors will readily tell you. They drafted and edited these stories, received detailed feedback from fellow Life Writers, and revised their narratives multiple times over several months. They worked hard and tweaked each sentence until it said what they wanted.

Our motto in Life Writers is *the only way to do this wrong is to not do it at all.*

If you feel inspired by these writers, join us at LifeWriters. us and receive the help you desire to create the story only *you* can write.

Patricia Charpentier
Owner/Founder
WritingYourLife.org
LifeWriters.us

My Life's Grand Prix

Norma Beasley

Larry, my next-door neighbor, is a walking encyclopedia on everything cars. His man cave is filled with over 250 die-cast stock cars and tons of memorabilia. His favorite race is NASCAR. Other than winning a race, it seemed pointless to me to go round and round a track until the checkered flag signaled a winner. But Larry pointed out to me some racing challenges. "Did it ever occur to you that drivers must utilize skill, endurance, and split-second strategizing?" he asked. Nope—never occurred to me. I returned home enlightened about racing and thought about the Monaco Grand Prix, which we had not discussed. Immediately, an analogy formed in my mind relating to turning points, life's twists and turns, and racing.

Vroom. Vroom. The Monaco Grand Prix begins a long, arduous, winding course through narrow city streets. There are elevation changes. Tight corners. Serpentine curves. Car problems. Low speeds at times. A wet track or oil or debris on the track from an accident. Even a tunnel that requires eye adjustments from daylight to darkness upon entering and exiting. The winner is determined by skill, focus, will, and endurance—the exact characteristics needed to meet life's challenges.

Note I did not say *problems* or *obstacles*. Words have power. When we speak of problems and obstacles, we revert to a negative mindset. Most of us pass the buck or throw our hands in the air, exclaiming, "I'm outta here." We have given up even before starting our journey of learning and embracing opportunities for growth and success. The Monaco Grand Prix reminded me of my journey in becoming a professional graphic designer and fine artist.

My first turning point in life began when I was orphaned at the age of two years old and placed in the loving care of my paternal grandma, Eva Beasley, who was a widow and had lost two sons to illness. She never uttered the words "You poor dear" to me. Life continued as though nothing out of the ordinary had happened. I had my grandma, and that's all that mattered.

When I was seven years old, she could no longer care for me, so I was passed to my maternal *grands*, Leiugania ("Lou") and Eugene Dooms. Granddad was the son of a slave yet became a restaurateur. Grandma was considered a well-educated woman and a talented seamstress. Two of her daughters were accomplished pianists, and to her way of thinking, it was a credible career that she wished to encourage me to pursue.

But I had other ideas. I was beginning to show signs of a budding artist. Paint-by-number sets and coloring books were my favorite pastimes. With dexterity of hand, I learned I could draw without the help of an art teacher. At the time I didn't know it, but my dad loved to doodle in his spare time. Maybe because she pushed too hard and had no respect for something I loved that originated deep within myself, Grandma and I locked horns. Granddad was content to let things play out, but Lou and I argued every day about my piano practice time. I hated to practice.

Finally, Granddad issued an ultimatum. "Norma, either you and my wife find a way to live in harmony, or you will have to leave this house."

I was stunned and not yet eighteen years of age. I knew he couldn't do anything legal about it, but still, angst hung in the air.

Then another turn of the road came my way. Reverend Alonzo Trigg, the community AME (African Methodist Episcopal) pastor, asked if I would be willing to babysit his young granddaughter while he and his wife attended a conference in Ohio.

"I'm not sure, Rev. Let me ask Granddad."

Granddad gave his blessing.

Upon Reverend Trigg's return, I asked if I could live with the family until I graduated from the University of West Virginia in approximately two years. The reverend gave his consent, and I left my grandparents' home, never to return.

The Triggs were a loving family, and I was ready to celebrate with a victory lap. In return for their kindness, I helped prepare meals, cleaned the church for Sunday service, helped around the house with everyday chores, and even played the piano for the church choir on Sundays! Reverend and Mrs. Trigg attended my graduation, but both sets of grandparents had passed away by then.

My next turn of events was the beginning of an art teaching career in Richmond, Virginia, but I first had to deal with the ugly fangs of racism. Potential employers looking for new employees at the university did not want to hire me because of my skin color. With the help of my teaching supervisor at the university, I was able to procure a position in the Richmond public school system. After one year of urban teaching, I decided to move to New York and earn my MFA degree in art at Pratt Institute, a prestigious private college in the Clinton Hill district of Brooklyn. Pratt students specialized in engineering, architecture, fashion design, fine arts, and interior and industrial design. My teaching professor at the university had told me, "Norma, if you ever have the chance to go to New York, apply to Pratt, the respected art school in Brooklyn. You will do well there."

Once again, a turn of events. Mrs. Trigg's brother, who lived in the Bronx, New York, invited me to stay with his family and continue my career in art. Full of excitement, I accepted the invitation and arrived at the Port Authority, an enormous transportation hub in Manhattan, at three o'clock one morning in June 1964. I telephoned Mr. Powell to pick me up. After arriving at his apartment in the Bronx, I struck out on my own and traveled to Queens to attend the World's Fair. I was too naïve to be fearful of the Big Apple, its subway trains, and its eight million people. My acceptance at Pratt meant a year of traveling two hours between Clinton Avenue in Brooklyn and 174th Street in the Bronx—not good at night as a woman traveling alone—which took a toll on me. I decided to relocate to Brooklyn.

I loved Brooklyn, with its private brownstone homes, numerous tree-lined streets, and suburban atmosphere. It was my cup of tea. The school helped me find lodging within walking distance with a Jewish landlady, Mrs. Rachel Webber, and her family, and I stayed with her until I earned my degree. She too attended my graduation.

In the meantime, I had to find a job and begin paying off school debt. To my delight, I found an opportunity listed in the *New York Times* and applied for an art clerical position in the Picture Collection of the New York Public Library in Manhattan. However, I did not want to make a career out of working in a library with few opportunities for advancement, so I looked for a more creative option every day during my lunch hour. Again, an ad in the *New York Times* offered an opportunity as an art editor with Harcourt, Brace & World, elementary school publishers. I was hired and remained with Mrs. Webber until I left New York in 1984 for Orlando, Florida, to continue my publishing career with now-named Harcourt Brace Jovanovich.

In 2003, I retired from the company as a managing art director. Thirty-five years at the helm of making learning fun for kids.

I had finished my journey with its twists and turns, won the checkered flag, and completed my life's grand prix.

The Fairmont Hairpin curve at Monaco through which Formula One cars race

NORMA BEASLEY

Norma Beasley is from the *Wild and Wonderful* state of West Virginia. She graduated from the University of West Virginia with a BA in art and from the Pratt Institute in New York with an MFA degree.

In 2003, Norma retired as a managing art director after thirty-five years of service with Harcourt Brace and Company, elementary education publishers specializing in curriculum development embracing the disciplines of math, reading, science, social studies, history, and health.

In 2019, the Florida Writers Association (FWA) selected Norma's memoir *Living Inside Out* as a semifinalist in the annual Royal Palm Literary Awards competition. The Florida Authors and Publishers Association awarded the memoir first place for cover design in 2020. Norma has written for FWA, the *Orlando Sentinel*, and the Rosicrucian Order, AMORC.

Norma also enjoys gardening, sports, photography, and travel. Currently, she is president of the Valencia Hills Homeowners Association and a district manager for the Rosicrucian Order, AMORC, in Florida.

"...And Gladly Teach":
Touching the Future

Terry Deer

"Are you free tomorrow? Martha needs help."

Two weeks before fall 2009 classes started, my housemate Steffi came home from preplanning at our church school to announce a call for volunteers to stuff envelopes.

On such fragile fulcrums do our lives turn.

We spent the next few days helping the office manager who, recognizing a fellow perfectionist, talked me into staying on as a volunteer after school opened and Steffi vanished into her seventh-grade English classes. Like Chaucer's Canterbury scholar, I would "gladly learn" at home amid the bustle of books and ringing bells. Provided no one asked me to take over a classroom, I was happy hanging on at the fringes.

Teaching was one profession I'd crossed off my list years before. I didn't have the temperament to be a disciplinarian. Far from *gladly* teaching, I couldn't imagine a worse fate than trying to keep the attention of a room full of children who would rather be anywhere else. Yet, without noticing, I became folded into the life of the school, making friends and learning faces. I relished the day the third-grade teachers invited me to tell stories to their students. I couldn't teach to save my life, but I felt confident as a storyteller. The children's rapt attention rewarded my efforts and justified my faith in storytelling as an effective means of crowd control.

7

Early the following spring, I missed the first cue to an impending change in my life.

Karen, the tall, autocratic head of school, swooped through the office one morning and found me at work. She paused, a stylish hawk hovering before a steep dive onto prey. I didn't yet realize I was the prey.

"Terry," she addressed me in her abrupt way, "you have a library degree, don't you?"

"Yes, from Chapel Hill," I replied, justly proud of my alma mater, although I didn't see where this was tending.

Karen gave me a brilliant smile and flew away on her original errand, choosing not to enlighten me. However, a few days later, our priest stopped me on the way out of the late service and handed me my second clue. "I've heard something good about you," he caroled, cheerful and imposing in his clerical garb.

"Oh?" As a member of the *frozen chosen*, an Episcopalian who sat in the back because there were no pews in the parking lot, I thought I'd done a good job of staying under his radar.

"It's a secret." He beamed.

Mathematics was not my strong point, but when the church rector, who happened to be married to the head of the church school, told me he'd heard something to my advantage, I could do the sum.

I wasn't surprised when Karen offered me a part-time position as school librarian.

Nevertheless, I hesitated over my answer. I'd be opening the library to twelve class visits a week—from kindergarten through fifth grade—a heavy load for two and a half days. I was already working part-time in the evenings at the community college library. *Would it be easier to teach library skills to kindergarteners than to show college freshmen how to use online databases?* I'd been a children's librarian in a public library, and I'd visited many schools as a storyteller. Surely this would be no different, and the income was welcome. So, I convinced myself and signed a contract in the deluded belief that experience with story times and book talks would be enough. I wasn't a teacher—didn't want to be a teacher, couldn't be a teacher—but I could run a library.

My first day of classes was a revelation. Nothing prepared me for the exhaustion. Five classes of wiggling, distractable children stomped through my quiet sanctuary and left it in tatters. I was dizzy from checking out books, fielding questions, cleaning up messes, and trying to put names to a hundred new faces. I closed the library door on my final class—fifth graders, some of them taller than I—and collapsed in tears.

In that moment, I understood that my training as a librarian was insufficient. I had to learn to be a librarian-teacher. Despite my lack of background or even affinity for the job, I had to master a new skill, almost a new language.

My students were happy to teach me. They taught me that a sense of humor would get me farther than a glare, that lesson plans were all very well, but sometimes the plans needed to go out the window, and that the most important thing I could teach them was that I cared.

I learned from Cole that a first grader might stumble across a word like *oviparous* and want to know what it meant. We looked it up together in the unabridged dictionary while he stood on a box to be tall enough. I learned from Sierra that cat-ear headbands are a valuable confidence booster and that you can be yourself even when you're not the same as anybody else. I learned from Austin that even a brief connection can leave a lasting mark. Austin, who would break my heart.

Austin stood out from the crowd of fifth graders—and not only because he was the tallest. He was a lanky, straw-blond handful of trouble, with a smile that bisected his face. Austin had no inhibitions and knew no shame, but beneath his boundless, exasperating energy was a good heart.

One Friday afternoon, Austin ambled into the library, flung himself on the rug, and proclaimed, "My grandma pranked me good today!"

Thank the Lord, I was forewarned, having already heard the story from his grandmother, one of the fifth-grade teachers. I rushed to grab the class's attention back before the irrepressible imp could continue. The day before, on the drive home from school, Carolyn had prepared Austin for his first sex-ed class by convincing him that puberty among young men began when a sensitive part of their anatomy fell off to reveal a new one growing underneath.

"Like baby teeth," she told him with a straight face.

Austin, electrified by this knowledge, couldn't wait to bring it up in class. When his grandmother confessed the hoax, he didn't believe her. I had to admire his courage in asking the question in front of all the boys in his grade. Even the realization that he'd been fooled didn't faze him; he delighted in the story. It remains my clearest memory of him.

Two years later, right before the start of his eighth-grade year, Austin died when he lost control of an ATV. The assistant head of school called to tell us. What a bitter duty he had, to shatter the peace of everyone on the faculty and staff, one person at a time. It was a brutal shock.

I couldn't wrap my mind around the loss. It was impossible that I'd never see Austin's cheeky grin again, never watch him saunter across the stage to receive his eighth-grade diploma.

I never thought I could lose one of my students.

Dazed by grief, the community gathered to mourn. We cried and told stories and laughed through our tears and hugged each other hard. The eighth graders built a court for *octoball*, a game he'd loved, and dedicated it to his memory.

Somehow, we carried on, though heavyhearted.

Austin's death taught me one more lesson. When I believed I didn't want to be a teacher, I misunderstood the calling. It wasn't, as I'd thought, about cramming unwanted knowledge into resistant heads. Teaching was about touching the future through the lives I touched in my library classes.

I'm not bold enough to think I had a part in guiding any of the young lives I encountered as a librarian-teacher, and yet my presence, my teaching, my stories, left a mark on them in the same way that Austin marked me. I can take pride in their accomplishments because I was part of the environment that helped to mold them. I cheer for Hayley when she lands a plum role on her way to a vibrant life in the theater. I marvel at Vicky, pouring her heart into researching clean energy. I pray for Myroslav, who was studying medicine in his native Ukraine when Russians invaded and who made the difficult choice to remain and help his people.

Austin should be among them. He should be here to experience all life has to offer—to make mistakes and live to learn from them. Denied that chance, he nevertheless changed the world. Children who never knew Austin now play octoball in the court that carries his name. Carolyn honors her grandson by giving her heart and efforts to each new class of fifth graders. Austin's friends, brought face-to-face with their mortality by the death that united them, forge their unique paths through life.

And I, a former teacher, tell the story of the day Austin's grandma pranked him good.

TERRY DEER

Terry Deer is a retired librarian and teacher who began life in Spokane, Washington. She has lived in nine of the contiguous states and one foreign country on her way to settling in Central Florida. She's been a writer since before she was ten, wrote fan fiction before it was cool, and is currently working on both a memoir of the years her family lived in England and a full-length fantasy novel. Terry recently published an article on the Folger Library in *The Shakespeare Oxford Newsletter*.

Besides words, Terry's passions include storytelling, the Shakespeare authorship question, cats, handwork, and jigsaw puzzles (alert readers may find at least one problem implied in that list). She currently lives in DeLand, Florida, with her close friend, Stephanie, and an undisclosed number of feline companions.

Last Words

Claudia Dickson

I have always been a strong, independent woman with a *glass-half-full* outlook on life. I always found the silver lining in all situations. I was the nurturer, the liaison, the problem-solver for all those around me. Life had thrown me many curveballs, but I always managed to scoop the ball up and toss it back into play. That was me.

Then it happened—COVID-19.

In ten days, my husband was gone.

After forty years, our intertwined lives were over. This curveball hit me smack in the face. I was no stranger to death. Over the span of ten years, I lost my father, my mother, my sister, and other significant friends. But this time was different. The next year would be a rollercoaster ride of lows and highs, obstacles, and uncontrollable emotions, taking me on a grief journey I never imagined. I was no longer the driver of my life.

Questions spun in my head. *Why did this happen? Could I have done something different? Who am I now? What will my life look like going forward? Will I ever be happy again?*

My days felt like a kaleidoscope, fragmented pieces coming together to form a picture. With one twist of the barrel, the pieces scattered and formed a new image. An endless variety of patterns. Chaos and fragile beauty merged momentarily. What the picture would look like next was a mystery.

My take-charge mind wanted to move through the grief quickly and put it behind me. Owning the struggle of letting go and allowing the process to take its own pace was burdensome. I sought out programs for those who had lost a loved one. Concern emerged when I met others who were stuck in their grief for many years. I didn't want that for me.

Along the way, I discovered that I was not alone and what I was feeling was normal. I chose to career head-on into my grief to push me through the tunnel to the other side, making my way to a new purposeful life.

Why do I tell you this? I share my encounters to help others find answers to the same questions. To instill hope. The journey of healing begins with leaning into your grief. You can't go around, over, or under—you must go through it. There is no expiration date on grief. You can try to hide from it or shelve it away, but it will be there when you least expect it if you don't deal with it, bearing its foulness in ways you never expected.

My journey was long, hard, and emotional. But I'm now back in the game and striving for home runs.

If you are asking yourself, "Can I find happiness again?" the answer is yes.

❧

The days following Jay's death were empty. I spent most of my time sleeping. When I was awake, I sat in my huge glass lanai of the new home we had purchased just two months before. It overlooked a semigreen lawn that was turning brown in preparation for its winter nap. A serene, wooded area sat behind it, and I watched the creatures who lived there. Birds swooped and played. Squirrels ran atop the length of the fence post. An occasional rabbit hopped across the lawn. Dragonflies fluttered back and forth before my eyes. I had never stopped long enough to notice.

Now, all I had was time. Lonely, empty time by myself. Alone. COVID-19 had made sure of that. No shoulder to cry on. No one to hug me. No one to just sit next to me on the couch and stare at the TV with.

Samantha and Joseph called me daily. I knew they were struggling with the loss of their father, but their calls were to check up on me. For the first time ever, I was too distressed to help them. I couldn't even help myself.

I found solace in talking about Jay. I reminisced for hours with those closest to me, smiling as I told my tales. Sometimes laughing, often crying. My cousin told me, months later, that she and her sister worried about my reaction to his death. They thought I was in shock. I didn't know it then, but they were right.

Shock comes in many forms. If someone had said that to me in the first three months, I would have said it wasn't true. I was fully aware (or so I thought) of what I was up against. I spoke frankly about our life together and Jay's death. *That's not what shock looks like, right?* I was dealing with it. How many people do you know who can have such a concise conversation about their loss so soon?

A couple of weeks in, I quietly emptied Jay's clothes closet into black bags and put them out in the garage for charity. I would hold onto them for several months, afraid of judging eyes condemning me for moving forward so quickly. But they were just things. Keeping them wouldn't bring him back.

After the dust had settled and all the funeral stuff was behind me, I had more spare time. That meant more time to think. My new existence was still surreal. I enjoyed the silence and I hated the silence.

A month after Jay passed, I received what I thought would be an ordinary call from my son.

"Hi, Mom. How are you doing?"

"I'm okay. I'm taking it a day at a time."

Normally, I would've been the one to ask that question, but now our roles were reversed. I don't even remember if I reciprocated the query.

"I have something to tell you, Mom."

"Yeah?"

"Kim and I are having a baby."

The words Jay had longed to hear for a lifetime.

Jay had talked incessantly about having grandchildren. He loved kids and took every opportunity to create happy memories with them. Baking cookies, playing games, taking them to fun places—our kids and everyone else's. His last words to me before he became incoherent were "I'll never meet my grandchildren."

I was speechless, trying to hold back the tears, but there was no stopping them. The waterworks gushed involuntarily from my eyes. I couldn't respond—no matter how hard I tried. Joseph waited on the other end silently. I heard Kim talking to him in the background.

"What did she say?"

"She's crying." I heard the mix of confusion, disappointment, and concern wrapped up in his response to her. He knew these weren't tears of joy.

I felt horrible that I had reacted so unexpectedly.

As I managed to get my crying under control, I said, "I'm sorry, Joseph. I didn't mean to take the joy out of your news. I'm really happy for you. It's just that all Dad ever wanted was grandchildren. I can't believe this is happening now."

"I know, Mom. We knew Kim was pregnant, but we were waiting for her to get through the first trimester before we shared the news with anyone."

I detected the sadness in his voice. How could he have known that Jay's time would be cut short so quickly?

"I understand, Joseph. Don't feel bad. I'm sorry you didn't get to tell him."

"Actually, I did tell him when you gave me the opportunity to speak with him over the phone before he passed."

By then, Jay had fallen into an unconscious state. I'd held the phone to his ear for a bit so Joseph could say whatever was on his mind. I hadn't listened. It was between them.

Now, I was glad Joseph shared this with me.

"I'm so happy to hear that, Joseph. They say the hearing is the last thing to go. I know he heard you."

I took a breath and let the news sink in—the way it was meant to be received.

"Wow, I'm gonna be a grandma."

CLAUDIA DICKSON

Claudia Dickson discovered her love of writing as a teenager growing up in Long Island, New York. In her early years, Claudia dreamed of writing and becoming a motivational speaker, but pursuing a dance career and raising a family left little time for writing. In 2017, Claudia retired to The Villages, Florida, with her husband, Jay. Three and a half years into retirement, Jay died of COVID-19 in 2020. This profound experience prompted Claudia to go after the dreams she held so many years before. She is currently working on her first book, *Who Needs Pennies from Heaven When You Can Have Quarters: A Journey of Grief and Healing.*

Wrong Way

Kit Dwyer

My parents had been out of the country for three years with my dad's work. Their decision to retire and move to Southern California now put them one thousand miles away from Colorado, where my husband, Dave, and I lived. Admittedly, it was a lot closer than Tokyo or Toronto, but having little vacation time from our jobs left us not visiting as often as I would have liked.

Dad and Mom showing us they found a Shakey's Pizza Parlor while living in Japan, 1979. "Imagine that!" they wrote on the back of the photo.

Phone calls between us were mostly brief, pleasant check-ins. Dad always rushed us off the phone. It was hard for them to break their fear of expensive long-distance charges, even though those no longer existed.

The summer my mom turned seventy-three, I answered my phone to hear her stumbling to find words. Her voice, usually sweet and caring, was an anxious whisper, quivering to catch back a breakdown of tears. What sounded like a minor husband-wife squabble made sense, but what didn't make sense was her sharing this with me at all. Our family norm was to keep charged emotions hidden. If someone in our family was having relationship problems, we usually didn't find out about it until the divorce papers were already filed. Discussing any ailments was also frowned upon. If someone were ill, it was never discussed in front of the children—until death was imminent.

"I can tell you're upset, Mom," I said. *Usually, she is giving me advice, not this way around.* "What are you going to do?"

"Well, I was wondering if it would be okay if I came to stay with you and Dave for a while. I mean, by myself. Without your father?" she asked.

My eyes widened. *My parents never do anything separately, except when Mom attends a religious retreat or a women's luncheon.* But I snapped my internal alarm bells closed like the lid on a travel clock. With fervor, I started daydreaming about what her long visit might be like. *I am sure Dave will think her visit is fine. Maybe we can deepen our mother-daughter relationship. I can show her my favorite places. We can go shopping together and attend plays and choral concerts.*

"We would love for you to come!" I exclaimed. "Do you want me to check on flight times?"

"No. Your father will drive us. And then he will return home," she said flatly.

I wasn't sure what to make of this. *Hopefully, Dad will explain later.*

Within the week, Dave and I greeted their arrival at our home. Dad had booked a flight back to California the next day. He would leave Mom with her own car to use during her stay with us. I could not see what emotions Dad was hiding. I avoided pressing for more information.

When alone on the drive to the airport, Dave asked Dad why he wasn't staying to visit longer with us. "Is there something wrong we should know about?"

Dad assured Dave there was no cancer or secret medical diagnosis. "Your mother-in-law is just upset with me over some things. She thought this trip was a good, temporary solution."

Clearly, this visit would be unlike any we had experienced before.

ॐ

In the weeks that followed, Mom gave us no details about her conflict with Dad. I assumed, with time, they would each lick their private wounds and come back to each other. So, we made plans for Mom's activities while Dave and I were at work. I helped her sign up for art classes at the local rec center, showed her a route to take our dog for walks, and entered ideas for weekend outings on our kitchen calendar.

Yet, something with Mom's mood was unmistakably off. Her natural curiosity and joyful exuberance seemed clouded by a veil. Her vim and vigor seemed to have vanished. She was shy about making decisions. At restaurants, Mom only ordered whatever we were ordering, and she had trouble picking an outfit to wear.

Mom also took in deep breaths and blew them out in long *whoosh* sighs, averting her eyes from us. *Maybe, I wondered, this breathing technique is something new she learned at church to help relieve anxiety. Dad isn't present right now, so there's no reason for her to feel worried or act subservient.*

Dad sent lengthy handwritten letters to Mom several times each week. She told us his letters were trying to smooth things over between them and that he wanted her to come home. I thought this would make her happy, but her mood did not improve. The letters kept coming.

One evening, Mom confessed to getting a traffic ticket for traveling the wrong way on a one-way street on the property of our local recreation center. Taking the ticket out of her purse, she slammed it down on the kitchen counter. "That stupid officer!" she shouted. "I told him those streets were not marked well! Why couldn't he just let it slide?" Tears filled her eyes, and her voice was shrill with angst. "I didn't hurt anyone or anything! He must have been sitting there, just waiting to give a ticket to someone for something!" Alternating one hand then the other, she began to pull on the hair of her forearms. "Don't tell your father."

I reached out and took her hand in consolation while Dave picked up the ticket and said calmly, "I'll take care of this."

A moment later, her expression fell to blank. The life in her eyes seemed to disappear behind an impenetrable fog.

In later phone calls with Dad, he told the story of Mom misplacing her car keys. He was angry because she would no longer talk about it with him. I knew that when Dad had too much to drink, he could become belligerent. It was easy to imagine their confrontation. Then Dad explained about stove burners left on and pantry items found in strange places. "After all," he half-joked, "it is just the two of us here. Who else could be doing those crazy things, except her? And why is she refusing to answer the phone when it rings? She doesn't make sense!"

I began to suspect something more than Dad's drinking needed attention. We were going to need help from outside our family.

Since my father refused to ever touch a computer, I was the one who started to research Mom's odd behaviors on the internet. We all longed to understand. I shared my findings almost daily by phone with Dad, and I mailed printed articles for him to read. In a couple of weeks, he agreed Mom should have a medical evaluation. I scheduled an appointment.

A devastating diagnosis of Alzheimer's disease left us reeling and terrified of the unknowns. As we read more and more about this affliction, we each sank into separate wells of emotional quicksand.

I can still see Mom shooting the basketball in our sunny driveway with our teenager, Ben. She was dodging about, laughing, and playing with her grandson on that day of clarity.

In a few more weeks, Dad came to Colorado to take Mom back to California in their car. Thankfully, she went willingly. Dad packed up the dozen or so items she had made in her pottery class, putting them in the trunk. He shook his head in bewilderment. "She is so creative, even with all this." We hugged and said pleasant goodbyes.

None of us talked to Mom about the diagnosis. We could not find the words. We never did find them.

Dad at our sink in Colorado, making his favorite sticky bun recipe, wearing Kit's favorite smile

Sharing the common tragedy between us seemed to bridge the physical distance. Dad and I became each other's sounding board, our fears buoyed by ideas about what was best to do next. But I knew Dad was the most alone with the sadness. He didn't have

Dave, Kit, Dad, and Mom, first Christmas in assisted living, 2004

as many distractions as I did with work and family. Even after they moved to Colorado to be near us, it was he who bore the heaviest weight of loss.

I never expected Mom's visit that summer would bene-fit my relationship with my dad. Over the coming years, my bond with my father would prove dearer to me than I ever could have imagined.

A day eventually came when Mom no longer recognized her husband at the table. The impact devastated my father so deeply that he stopped eating and, within a month, passed away.

The journey we traveled together feels like a tattoo seared on my memory—unless my memory, too, becomes obscured behind some approaching fog, something that turns my mind a wrong way.

KIT DWYER

Kit Dwyer originates from rural Pennsylvania. She has been authoring poems, letters, and essays since third grade. After retiring from a project management career in the GIS (computer mapping) industry, she discovered her love of audio recordings and now helps her personal history clients record their life stories.

Kit currently lives in Stone County, Missouri, with her husband, Dave, and their third English springer spaniel, Scout. In addition to writing, Kit also takes pleasure in adventures with her two grandchildren, volunteering with community projects, weaving, going kayaking, and hiking. You can read more about Kit and her work at FirsthandMemories.com.

Iowa Braille School

Lucille Ellson

By happenstance, I took a job teaching at the Iowa Braille School. Floyd and I had planned for me to stay home with the children until they started college. Then, I would begin teaching again. I signed a contract to teach third grade in the East Elementary School in Vinton, but after two years, I had colon cancer surgery and left teaching for two years.

Before I signed the contract to return to teaching, a friend of mine, Fran Rector, a third-grade teacher at the Iowa Braille School, came to me and said she was changing jobs, and there would be a vacancy there if I were interested. She explained the pros and cons of the job and stressed that it would be easier physically—no playground duty and the school limited the class size to no more than ten students. Fran also said this was a good year to try the Braille School as there would be two third-grade classes, one reading large print while learning Braille and the other only in Braille for students who already knew how to interpret the series of raised dots.

Lucille's Braille School students

By third grade, public school students with poor vision and their parents realized they could no longer keep up reading in print and needed to attend the Iowa Braille School. This made for an influx of third-grade students, creating the perfect time for me to try a new teaching adventure. I would be able to use large print books as well as teaching Braille to the students while becoming more proficient myself.

ॐ

The Iowa Braille School was under the supervision of the Iowa Department of Public Instruction. Each summer on the Vinton campus, it provided a session run by the University of Northern Iowa to help qualify Braille teachers. The first summer, I took classes in Braille I and Orientation of the Blind.

The Braille writing system starts with the Braille cell, which is made up of six raised dots in two columns of three dots each. Besides the letters of the alphabet, the code also includes punctuation marks, contractions, abbreviations, and such. Braille has at least 250 different arrangements when used for higher mathematics and music. To read Braille, students must eventually memorize most of these combinations. Not only that, but their fingertips need to be trained to feel and distinguish the dots.

I marveled at how well most of the students learned to read Braille. Their fingers glided over the dots quickly. I had the advantage of seeing

A B C D E F G H I J

K L M N O P Q R S T

U V W X Y Z 1 2 3 4

5 6 7 8 9 0 . , # space

Braille alphabet

Lucille Ellson

the dots, so I never reached a high level of proficiency in reading the dots by touch.

Each student also had a Braille writer that resembled a typewriter and was used to write in Braille. It was clumsy to carry around, so the students also learned how to write Braille using a slate and a stylus. This was pocket-sized and became

Reading a Braille book

their pencils and papers. The slate was a hinged metal device about 8.5 inches, the width of a sheet of paper, and composed of four to six rows of Braille cells of six small openings. The vision-impaired student put a sheet of thick paper in the slate and pressed the stylus through the holes to create raised dots to form letters and words. In the third grade, students also learned how to write on a typewriter, which made it possible for them to communicate with sighted people.

∞

I taught at the Iowa Braille School for fourteen years and had all kinds of new experiences while working with blind students. One involved learning to cope with the different mannerisms they developed to compensate for their lack of sight. Students used their sense of hearing to listen to music, a worthwhile and enjoyable pastime. Many of them walked around campus carrying a small radio tuned in to their favorite music.

They also loved listening to all other sounds and figuring out ways to mimic them. One little boy found a set of keys that made a tinkling noise he liked, so he attached these to his wrist. It did not take long before most of the class carried rings of keys to enjoy the jingling sound made as they walked.

I didn't ask where the keys came from. I was sure some parents missed a key or two. Keys finally had to be banned in the classroom because of the noise created from all the jingling.

Another sound that annoyed me was the constant tapping of a foot on the floor. Upon hearing those first few taps, I offered the student a piece of foam rubber to put under his or her foot. That stopped the tapping because the foam mat embarrassed them. Others made odd noises with their mouths or rhythmic sounds by tapping pencils on their desks.

Students developed varying mannerisms. Poking or pushing in her eyeballs gave one little girl a pleasurable sensation. They often pulled or twisted their hair until bald spots appeared. Sally always *scrubbed* people, which meant she ran her fingers up and down their bodies to learn something about them. Most pupils liked to rock back and forth in their desks, especially if the desks made little squeaks.

My job involved stopping or diminishing these behaviors to help students fit in better with the sighted world.

৪০

A totally blind student had no concept of what a sighted person saw. Students walked through a long tunnel from the dorm to the classroom. Some of the younger boys began playing too much along the way and arrived after the tardy bell rang. To put a stop to this, the principal made a rule that if a student arrived late, he would have to visit her office.

I always left my classroom door open until all the pupils had arrived. One morning, Jason walked backward into the room. When I asked why he was walking backward, he answered, "Because I heard the tardy bell. I didn't want you to see me and send me to the principal's office."

The school put Braille writers in the dorm for the students to use, but the special Braille paper, which was thicker than ordinary paper, was handed out sparingly by the house-mother. Jerry decided to help himself to the classroom supply of paper and stood in line to walk to the dorm while holding the sheets behind his back. I said to him, "What are you holding behind your back, Jerry?"

He replied, "How can you see behind my back? I didn't want you to see that paper."

Obviously, blind students didn't comprehend what sighted people can see, and I had to teach that concept to them.

ༀ

Braille School teachers had duties not expected of public schoolteachers. We ate lunch with the students and were expected to help them acquire good table manners. The students learned that meat was placed at twelve o'clock on their plates and vegetables at six o'clock. Half a slice of bread was used as a *pusher* to eliminate using their fingers to get food onto the fork or spoon.

A weekend duty we teachers didn't especially enjoy was transporting students who lived near Vinton to the Greyhound bus station on Friday after school and then picking them up on Sunday. Teachers were assigned this duty once a month.

Every three weeks, all students visited their homes. The school's buses drove in all directions in Iowa where parents picked up their children at specified meeting locations. A few children had to ride 150 miles or more to get home. The buses left at noon on these Fridays with a sack lunch for each child and a caregiver in charge. Occasionally, for various reasons, some students couldn't go home, so teachers often had a student or two as weekend guests.

Also on weekends, teachers took turns assisting the recreational instructor. This meant helping at the bowling alley, swimming pool, gym, and such. The children often went on field trips to parks, museums, large department stores, etc. To keep the students from wandering off, they hung onto a long rope with an adult on each end.

&

The students and the entire community looked forward to the creative, fun, and emotional Christmas programs produced by Jerry Kakac, the school's vocal music teacher. Much work, time, and thought went into the stage sets and costumes, and each teacher was required to make the costumes for their students. This made for a busy season with teachers sewing elf, angel, toy, or candle costumes—whatever the production's theme needed. We also helped our classes with the stage settings, such as making Santa's sleigh or a chimney out of cardboard and painting them. The joy and excitement these Christmas programs gave the blind children touched everyone's heart, and I felt well rewarded for the extra work required.

&

This story came full circle for me when I read the November 11, 2022, edition of the Vinton *Cedar Valley Times*. I felt surprised to see a picture of Raymond Lough, one of my fully blind third-grade students who had been elected as Benton County Attorney. Raymond was just one of my amazing students.

Looking back on my fourteen years of teaching at the Iowa Braille and Sight Saving School, I now cherish the wonderful memories, the amazing students and teachers, and the knowledge I gained there.

LUCILLE ELLSON

Lucille Ellson grew up on the family farm near Laurens, Iowa, with two sisters and four brothers. She rode to school in a horse-drawn bus for her first two years.

After graduating from the University of Northern Iowa, which was then called Iowa State Teachers College, Lucille's teaching career included eight years in Iowa public schools and fourteen at the Iowa Braille and Sight Saving School in Vinton, Iowa.

Lucille and her husband, Floyd, coauthored his memoir, *My First Hundred Years,* which was completed and published in 2016, several years after Floyd's death. Her memoir, *My Last Hundred Years and Change*, was written by Lucille and her son Jim and published in 2023. Floyd and Lucille were both centenarians when they wrote their life stories.

Lucille lives in Orlando, where she and Floyd moved after their retirement.

After sixty-nine years of marriage, Floyd passed away in 2012.

A Change of Scenery

Julie Folkerts

When I married my husband, Don, an only child with blond hair and blue eyes, and after moving fifty-plus times at that point in my life, I realized it might be possible to live in the same place for more than a few months. Don grew up in Kansas in the same house, had the same neighbors, same friends, and same school for seventeen years, along with family living around the corner. Something I never knew or experienced.

Excited by the prospect of building stronger relationships, I began dreaming of a utopia. I soon realized there was no real utopia, but at least I might get close. I could develop real bonds, know the streets I traversed, the parks I walked, the stores I frequented, and the neighbors I lived next to, giving me a feeling of belonging.

All my life, the anxiety and uncertainty of not knowing where our next stop might be, or if I would find a friend, had constantly remained on my mind. The main concern I have always had—to be accepted.

The moves started after my parents met as members of the same ski club on the mountain slopes of Colorado and married in 1957. With only a high school education, Dad tried his hand at many odd jobs, all of which fell short of his ambition and drive. Shortly after marrying my mom, Dad was hired as a permanent employee with the United States Geological Survey in USGS's Topographic Division, Rocky

Mountain Region, headquartered in Lakewood, Colorado. They assigned him various projects within the seven-state area of Montana, North Dakota, South Dakota, Wyoming, Colorado, New Mexico, and Texas. Before the oil pipeline was built in the 1970s, he worked with the survey crew that mapped Prudhoe Bay, Alaska.

Other families were also a part of the Rocky Mountain Region and moved as we did, with several projects finding us in the same cities; therefore, developing a bond, we called ourselves a "survey family." We went to the same schools and spent time at each other's homes.

One incident found me standing face-to-face with Tammy, also my age, protecting our siblings over some misunderstanding. The cli-

Survey family visiting Canada

max occurred when Tammy grabbed my long blond hair, forcing me to the ground. Fighting erupted—with nails coming out—while our siblings yelled. Our mothers heard the commotion and quickly interceded before things got out of hand.

Dad's first assignment took us to Wyoming, the beginning of many moves over his thirty-year career. From the time I was a year old, Dad's job required us to move two to three times per year. This transient lifestyle made it difficult to produce long-lasting friendships. Making pen pals along the way, eventually, like the saying "out of sight, out of mind," we lost track of each other and stopped communicating. Following

Julie Folkerts

our frequent moves was a challenging task for any young person. But I continued to make new friends and found other interests.

My oldest friend, Robyn, and I still communicate to this day. In Montana, we were freshmen in high school together. Fond memories remain of meeting her in June 1972 while playing summer volleyball in the school gym. Coincidently, we both played the trumpet in the band and were elected by our classmates to serve as homecoming duchesses. Memories flourish of riding atop a red convertible, waving to onlookers in our formal gowns, long hair flowing in the breeze during the Harlowton High School Homecoming Parade.

Robyn and I have remained friends through our challenges in life. She and her husband visited us in Denver after both of our marriages. Seeing each other and meeting the men we chose to marry was exciting. Several years later, a horrific accident claimed the life of Robyn's husband. Upset and unsure of what to say to Robyn, it took me some time to pick up the phone and share my condolences.

I learned that, as an adult, if your friend meant a lot to you and vice versa, you would never forget them. You might not speak regularly, but they remain in your heart.

These kinds of friendships last forever. I try to remind these friends at Christmas by sending a short letter affirming that I continue to cherish their friendship. I mail over seventy-five Christmas cards to family and friends during the holidays. When I disclose the large number I send out, I am continually asked how I have so many people to send cards to. My reply remains the same: I want to keep in contact with these people as they have touched my heart along the way.

Being a part of a family means the world to me. With my family's transient lifestyle, I only saw my grandparents, aunts, uncles, and cousins when we moved—north in the summer and south in the winter. With USGS headquarters in Lakewood, Colorado, a suburb of Denver, it was a necessary stop for Dad to turn in his completed assignment and pick up the next one. Most of my extended family lived there.

Mapmaking today is not conducted as it was in the 1950s to 1970s. Now digitized, there is no need for cartographers and their families to move around from place to place, working from aerial photographs. When men like my father surveyed Alaska, no families accompanied them because of the weather conditions and the fact that the men lived

Dad in Alaska at his tent camp

in tents with handmade latrines. Below, I've shared a picture of my dad in Alaska near those living conditions.

Each move carried with it an adjustment period. The weather in the next location was one question. Since most of Dad's work was conducted outside, the weather was a significant factor.

Living quarters were another important consideration. As we pulled into each new location, Dad introduced himself to a gas station attendant or motel clerk or asked any local if they knew of available rental space, preferably furnished. This frequently led to the rental of a trailer, apartment, duplex, or house we could call home for a four- to six-month stay.

After locating housing, reluctantly, we needed to thoroughly clean before unpacking; some properties hadn't been lived in for years. Often, the house only had one bedroom and a screened-in porch. My sister would get the couch, and I, the oldest daughter, called the porch my bedroom. There were times when my sister and I slept in sleeping bags on aluminum cots. Several locations required us to move twice when the landlords sold the properties we were renting. We even lived in an apartment above a general store in Wyoming and in a twenty-foot travel trailer in Montana.

It was a balancing act to settle into the rental space, enroll my sister and me in school, and locate new doctors. Mom wanted us to feel special on the first day at the new school, so as soon as we found her sewing machine, she busied herself sewing new dresses.

A people person of sorts, I enjoyed making new friends. But the most challenging part was the initial introduction at the front of the classroom in grades one through six, where I invariably heard the hurtful words *bucky* or *beaver teeth* from a couple of students. I tried to act like I didn't hear their words as the teacher guided me to my desk. I had sucked my thumb until the age of six and had the overbite to confirm it. I patiently waited for the day the braces would go on at age twelve.

I was fortunate to be a good student, so taking me in and out of different classes every few months proved to be only a small challenge. My induction into the National Honor Society as a junior in high school resulted in one of my dad's favorite moments. He worried that moving around so extensively would cause issues with our education and that we wouldn't get credit for unfinished classes.

For the last two years of high school, my mother decided to stay put so my sister and I could have some consistency.

Julie (left) and family at The Alamo in San Antonio, Texas

Dad continued to move, only coming home periodically, although, in the summer months, we traveled north with him to cooler weather.

During all these moves—forty-five before I graduated from high school—I met many new and different friends along the way and enjoyed all the contrasting scenery and landscaping. From the White Sands of New Mexico to the Black Hills of South Dakota, from the Gulf Coast of Texas to the Rocky Mountains of Colorado, extensive inspiring scenery can be found across this region of the United States.

I want to share these adventures with friends and family, as I have been repeatedly asked to do over the years. Sharing small amounts of my life with others encouraged me to begin writing my memoir. My parents are gone now, but the memories and adventures will remain in my heart and mind forever.

JULIE FOLKERTS

Julie Folkerts is a recent breast cancer survivor and a retired legal assistant with a bachelor of business administration degree from Texas Woman's University. Over her twenty-five-year career, she worked for several law firms in Denver, Dallas, and Houston.

Born in Denver, Colorado, Julie, at the age of one, began moving with her family two to three times per year for her father's career as a cartographer for the United States Geological Survey. Currently, Julie is writing her memoir about the places and people she and her family encountered along the way. In addition, she writes a weekly blog with a steadily growing readership at www.Goodbye-Girl.com.

Julie, a mother of two grown daughters, is passionate about helping others. She enjoys quilting and scrapbooking besides reading and writing. She lives with her husband in Katy, Texas.

Camping Lessons

Millie Ford

I grew up on the south side of Chicago in an abandoned shack of a neighborhood. The one sliver of light shining through the broken boards was the community center, Benton House. With a postage stamp park across the street, it provided a respite to children growing up with limited green space. They organized after-school sports, provided arts and crafts classes, and offered homework assistance. During the summer, all-day programs included field trips to museums, cooking classes, and outings to a nearby pool. Anything to keep us from opening the fire hydrants.

The summer after I turned ten, Benton House offered a three-night camping trip for the fifth- and sixth-grade girls and boys. I had never camped before, and I thought it would be fun. The only problem was how to get permission and money from my mother. She already paid the fee for the summer day session, but this would be an extra charge. I would ask her when she got home from work.

We didn't have air-conditioning in our apartment, and that night, it was steamy. The backs of my legs stuck to the vinyl-covered kitchen chair. My knee bounced up and down, and my mother was silent, holding a wet wash rag to her neck. "I want to go," I mumbled as I inched the camp information and permission slip across the table. "It's only fifteen dollars. Sharon is going and—"

"I don't care what Sharon is doing," my mother shouted, barely lifting her eyes to look at the sheet of paper. "I have to be mother and father. You think money grows on trees. I don't have fifteen dollars lying around. What did I pay these people for?" The litany continued.

My mother's whole body tightened. She pushed the paper across the table with enough force that it landed on the floor. I knew I would get nowhere with her. I would unleash more fury if I continued talking, so I made a quick and silent exit to my room.

There, I counted the money I had. Even though I was only ten, I had saved money from babysitting, birthdays, and coins found on the ground or forgotten in pay telephones. I counted it, and I had enough to pay for the trip. My mother didn't want me to go, but I didn't want to miss out on this experience with my friends. I never had a vacation before, and I wanted an adventure. *She said she doesn't have the money, so if I do, then it should be okay. Right?* My logic muscle was starting to develop.

But today would not be the day to tell my mother I intended to go. I waited for the perfect moment: before she left for work, when she wasn't running late, and when it wasn't too hot in the apartment to make her uncomfortable. The days ticked by, and soon it was the day before the bus would depart. I had to tell her. I summoned all the courage I could and bravely announced, "I have the money. I'm going to camp."

"I don't give a shit what you do," she spat back.

Not the best day after all.

The next morning, I forged her signature on the permission slip and found a suitcase in the closet. I knew nothing about packing, but I threw together the clothes I thought I would need.

My mother was gone before I left. No kiss goodbye, no "be careful," just a slammed front door. An hour later, I shoved my money and forged document in my pocket, grabbed my suitcase, and walked out the door.

It was a hot, humid, late-July day when I started my journey. Six blocks to freedom. Six blocks and many anxious steps to the community center. My suitcase was heavy, my hand was sweaty, and I had to stop every so often to change hands. When my hand slipped, the side of the suitcase hit my shins.

I was halfway to the community center when I came to the street where my best friend, Sharon, lived. I knew her mom would help me, but I was too embarrassed to ask. I walked on the other side of the street. *If my mom really cared, she would walk me to camp, sign the permission slip in person, and pay the fee.*

Instead, I was hot and sweaty when I got there. The woman behind the desk said nothing as she counted my crumpled bills and the change stuck to my hand. I was convinced I'd be arrested for forgery, but once again, the woman said nothing.

I safely escaped a life behind bars and jumped on the bus. The boys collected at the back, and the girls took the seats upfront. We sang songs, played cat's cradle, and giggled in the high-pitched, squeaky voices of preteens.

We arrived at camp after lunch and spent the afternoon playing outdoor games like dodgeball and red rover. Before dinner, we were assigned cabins. I was bunking with Sharon, Diane, and Mary Ann. Sharon wanted the top bunk, and I was glad to oblige. I was certain if I slept on the top bunk, I'd fall out of bed.

Even though it was muggy, the air pressure at camp felt lighter. I wasn't under my mother's oppression and constant harping. I could make noise and be silly, just like my friends. After a dinner of spaghetti and meatballs in the mess hall, it was time to settle into our cabins for the night.

The first night at camp, the girls in my cabin would see I didn't bring the right stuff. Embarrassment washed over me before I even opened my suitcase. We only had one tube of toothpaste at home, and I knew I couldn't take it, so I brought a carton of Arm & Hammer baking soda in a plastic produce bag. To hide my shame of not having someone who cared enough to help me pack, I put on my smarty-pants hat and explained the science behind baking soda and oral hygiene. *What a dork*, I thought as I fell asleep.

The morning of the third day, we packed up our stuff and boarded the bus taking us to the second location, the camp where we would sleep in the tents and sleeping bags provided to us. After we arrived, we swam in a river and enjoyed the outdoors. Or, at least, some of us did. My pale skin was sunburned, and I discovered mosquitos liked their meals crispy. My fiery skin itched.

After dinner, we sat around a campfire and made s'mores. Boys, feeling the burgeoning strength of their ten and eleven years, launched toasted marshmallows into the air. One landed in my stringy long blonde hair. My friends tried to get it out, but their sticky fingers made it worse. Just as we finished our s'mores, it began to rain, and we retreated to our tents.

There were four of us in the tent. Later in the night, when the boys should have been asleep, the marshmallow-throwing thugs pulled the posts out from the girls' tents. Rain-soaked tents landed on us. Our sleeping bags were drenched, and we couldn't get back to sleep. It rained through the morning.

The camp counselors tried to make breakfast, but with the rain, it was impossible to keep the campfire going. I stomped up to a counselor as she struggled with the fire. "Can we please go now?" I asked. "Everyone is miserable."

Instead of eggs and toast, we ate peanut butter on cold white bread. Finally, back on the bus, we started to dry out.

Most of us slept the whole way home. I'm sure the camp counselors appreciated the quiet. Back at the community center, they invited us to stay until our designated pickup time since our parents didn't know we had arrived home early. (Life without email and texting was simple yet complicated.)

I'd had enough of camp—the snapshot days too familiar and easy to forget, the boys who did anything for attention, and the counselors who were clearly in over their heads. I would walk home. No one was coming to get me. I was tired but fine. I wasn't sure what I'd face when I got home, but I had a few hours before my mother would return from work. I had enough time to figure it out.

So, what did my fifteen dollars buy? Sunburn, mosquito bites that swelled into hives, and melted marshmallow in my hair. But it also brought a small sip from the fountain of freedom. An understanding that sometimes I needed to remain silent, sometimes I needed to speak up, and sometimes I needed to walk the path alone to become the person I was meant to be.

MILLIE FORD

Millie Ford has returned to writing after a successful career in retail marketing. Her writing is known for its unique imagery and powerful metaphors. She is currently working on a series of essays she hopes can become a memoir. In addition to writing, Millie is passionate about animal rescue. She volunteers at a local animal shelter to help stray animals get adopted into loving homes. Millie lives in the Chicagoland area with her rescue cat, Isaac. One of her essays will be published in *Storytellers' True Stories About Love, Volume 2,* by Chicago Story Press in 2023.

All in a Day's Blindness

Deborah Hunt Repp

I went blind in one eye on a Tuesday. I was thirty-two, single, living in Manhattan, and a well-paid executive secretary to the president. Life was good. On that particular day in January 1981, I taxied from my West Side Manhattan apartment to the office on Forty-Sixth and Park Avenue. By 8:30 a.m., the president and top management were sequestered in their board of directors meeting.

In the linoleum-tiled lunchroom, I poured a cup of coffee and greeted other early workers. Turning left to the executive area, I walked on thick, light blue wool carpet to my desk chair where I eased myself into it.

"Good morning, Diane. How was your commute from New Jersey?" She looked up, smiling, and nodded to me. Diane was in her thirties and well-groomed with short black hair. Secretary to the corporate attorney, she had responsibility for board meetings and was busy with paperwork.

At my desk, I arranged my calendar, spiral notebook, and coffee to be ready for action. Fellow secretaries strolled to their desks: four ladies at mahogany desks to my left and four to my right. Our day began.

By ten a.m. I completed yesterday's to-do list but felt nauseated and a bit shaky. I thought it might be the coffee and not eating a good breakfast when a sudden, sharp pain in my jaw nearly doubled me over. I stood up, recovered, and had the presence of mind to walk into Mr. Foster's office to be out of sight from my colleagues. I smoothed my skirt and, leaning forward, tottered to one side. I almost fell over but recovered just as quickly, steadying myself on my feet as I outstretched a hand along the wall and walked back to my desk.

I sat down slowly and felt safe in my chair. Closing my right eye, I covered it with my right hand and stared down the row of secretaries to my right. I blinked my left eye and saw only a milky, translucent white. Keeping calm and professional, I covered my left eye with my left hand while staring down the same row with my right eye. Diane's red dress was clear as day. I switched hands and eyes, back and forth, and realized I had no vision in my left eye—only snow-white blindness.

Something is wrong.

I walked to Diane, leaned over, and into her ear whispered, "I don't think I can see very well."

Diane swiveled in her chair to face me and clasped my hand. I stood beside her and repeated the eye exercise. The drama at Diane's desk attracted my coworkers, who gathered beside us. I felt confused but maintained my composure. I took deep breaths, clenched my teeth, and reaffirmed myself: *I am a smart, levelheaded woman with Midwest common sense.*

"Debbie, you need an eye doctor, and you need one now," Diane insisted.

My mind raced through my Rolodex.

"Oh, I know Dr. Smith, an optometrist where Mr. Foster goes. I'll call him," I said to the group.

I explained the sudden blindness to Dr. Smith's receptionist.

"Come to the office immediately," she said, and I hung up the phone.

"I'm going to an optometrist," I announced to the secretaries within earshot. "I'll call Diane when I know something."

Passing Diane, I mumbled, "Please tell Mr. Foster what's happened to me and where I've gone." I tossed on my coat and clenched my purse.

"Good luck," my friends chimed.

Outside the building and the security of the office, I realized I must turn my head left to get the entire picture. Spring-cool outside, clear, about forty-five degrees—I sucked in a chilly breath. My high heels clomped a steady marching staccato on the pavement, distracting me from confused thoughts. I turned my head fully left. Heavy traffic from Grand Central Station's ramp always shot through the light there. I judged traffic, then quickly crossed the intersection at Forty-Sixth and Park.

Now, eleven o'clock, surrounded by canyons and layers of concrete gray, granite, and darkened reflective glass, I felt small. At Madison, I continued south to Forty-Fourth to the middle of the block and the optometry office of Dr. Smith.

I quickly filled out necessary paperwork for the receptionist. After five minutes, Dr. Smith stood beside my chair. He was a tiny fellow, fiftyish, with a clean and tidy appearance. We briefly discussed my background and condition as we walked into his exam room. I felt a calm aura around the doctor. Surrounded by optical equipment, he began a routine exam as if I were here for eyeglasses. He repeated one test.

Afterward, Dr. Smith quietly said, "Deborah, there is nothing I can do for you. Your next step is to see an ophthalmologist. I'll make an appointment for you." He stepped out of the room and, within five minutes, returned to hand me an address card. "Good luck at the ophthalmologist."

All in a Day's Blindness   **51**

Outside, I jumped into a taxi headed north. Traffic was light on Madison. By 11:45 a.m., I entered Dr. John Hines' office at Eightieth and Park Avenue. Befitting this high-rent district on the Upper East Side, his waiting area was large with several chairs and couches in muted beige and blue fabric. After thumbing magazines for two hours, I called Diane.

"Just me, Diane. I'm at Eightieth and Madison, an ophthalmologist. More tests and still blind. I won't be back today."

She assured me everything was under control with the board of directors. "I briefed Mr. Foster. He was very concerned."

"Yeah, me too. Let him know I will call him at home later tonight."

I returned to the magazines and noticed my entire body was firing uncomfortable tingles. It felt as if the Milky Way was exploding under my skin. Those electric charges of celestial firecrackers exhausted me further. I could not read anymore.

Abruptly, the bodily tingles stopped.

The receptionist called my name.

Over the next half hour, Dr. Hines gave me routine eye tests. His nurse then administered more ophthalmological tests, including a field-of-vision test within a white dome with flashing lights, and next, I arranged colored blocks to show the hues like in a rainbow gradation test. The dome's flashing light was the most tiring, but making a color rainbow out of one hundred blocks was tedious.

Finally, at four thirty, Dr. Hines informed me gently, "Well, your optic nerve is compromised, Deborah. I can do nothing here. I've called Doctor Randall, a neurologist affiliated with Mount Sinai Hospital. He is waiting in his office at

Ninety-Fifth and Fifth. I called a taxi for you, which is waiting outside on the curb. I'll walk you out."

Ten minutes later, I met Dr. Randall. He was tall, meticulously dressed, and with clean fingernails that drummed his cherrywood desktop. We briefly talked in his formal office. Obviously, Dr. Hines prepped him by phone.

In the exam room, I undressed to my bra and panties as instructed and covered myself with a sheet. In a moment, Dr. Randall knocked and entered the room alone, as his staff had left for the day. Cool and detached, he methodically began a thorough neurological exam: knee, elbow, and ankle thumps with a joint reflex hammer; skin pinpricks all over my entire body with a sharp needle; audible sounds from a tuning fork in my ear; balance and strength tests of my limbs being pushed and pulled; and following his moving finger with my sight. When he finished, Dr. Randall asked me to dress.

I returned to his office after the exam, the most grueling so far, and sat across from him at his desk. *Here it comes*, I thought. I folded cold hands and waited for the verdict, feeling none of the warmth and kindness I felt from the previous two doctors.

"Deborah, I'm allowed three emergency patients at Mount Sinai in a week. I'd like you to check in there at One Hundredth and Fifth by ten tomorrow morning for tests: a spinal tap, more eye exams, and maybe a water temperature test, so you might bring a bathing suit. Is that satisfactory?"

"Of course, Doctor Randall, but what is wrong with me?" I pleaded.

He answered matter-of-factly. "There are several possibilities, but I will have more information after hospital tests. Just go home and rest. Call and arrange your life because you'll be in the hospital until Friday. I'll see you during my afternoon rounds. We'll go from there."

I pulled my belongings together and quickly left his office, feeling it more like an escape than an exit. Once on the sidewalk, everything hit me: the dirty smell of exhaust fumes and the bumper-to-bumper, frightening honking of rush-hour traffic. The cold night air draped me with penetrating aloneness. I eventually hailed a taxi to take me across Central Park to the West Side, arriving safely at my building on Sixty-Fourth and Broadway. I paid the last fare of another five bucks and climbed out of the back seat with help from my doorman. I was exhausted and scared. I wanted to talk to my parents.

Secure within my dark one-bedroom apartment and turning on enough light to navigate, I opened a cold Coke, grabbed a sleeve of Ritz crackers, and sat on my queen-sized bed. I gently raised the turquoise princess phone to my ear and dialed my parents in Iowa. It was seven o'clock in New York.

At the comforting sound of Mother's voice, I rattled off my terrifying news in run-on sentences. "Hello, Mother, it's me—I'm finally in my apartment after three doctors! The last one's throwing me into Mount Sinai for tests tomorrow until Friday. I'm still blind since I phoned this morning—I've had every eye test imaginable—and I don't know a damn thing yet."

I burst into tears, knowing my life would never be the same.

DEBORAH HUNT REPP

Deborah Hunt Repp grew up on a farm in rural Iowa. She completed high school and college with a BA in accounting. Next on her agenda was secretarial training at the prestigious Katharine Gibbs Secretarial School in Boston (now closed).

Eventually, Deborah worked for top management at several worldwide New York City–based corporations. Despite acquiring multiple sclerosis, she worked for twenty-five years, enjoying the whirlwind excitement of city life. With her cheerful outlook, she traveled on five continents both before and while dealing with MS.

Retired and farming in the Midwest, Deborah enjoys learning and traveling with friends and family. Arts, world cultures, history, architecture, and museum exhibitions are what attract Deborah most in her travels.

Unconditional Love

Etya Krichmar

The love between mother and child happens naturally from conception when an umbilical cord unites two bodies and souls. Some call it unconditional and eternal.

I accepted love as a natural feeling by being fortunate to be born into a loving family and assumed every child had a right to be loved by the person who gave them life. I didn't associate the love I received from Mama with any words.

When I came to the United States of America, for the first time in my life, I heard the expression "unconditional love." It took some years for me to understand its meaning.

Growing up in the Soviet Union, I was unaware of this phrase. In Russian, the term *bezgranichnaya luybov* comes close to the description of unconditional love. The exact translation of these two words is love without borders, which may mean something different in English.

The USSR's harsh reality of living left little room for the words *bezgranichnaya luybov* to be used as a daily lexicon. Russians, the stoic people under the totalitarian regime, couldn't afford the luxury of dwelling on personal feelings. They struggled to survive. We learned about love by watching our parents treat us with kindness.

Love lived inside the home where I grew up. Being poor didn't stop our family from being human, but this wasn't the case for some of my friends living in abusive, dysfunctional families. Their lives were filled with horrors.

Etya and her daughter   Etya and her son

It is no wonder I didn't use the words *unconditional love* to describe what I felt when I became a mother for the first time at twenty-one. I only knew I would gladly die for my daughter as I held her in my arms.

Nine years later, my precious son was born. When the doctor cut the umbilical cord to separate our physical bodies, I sensed an invisible thread replacing it, connecting us for eternity. It didn't feel like separation because this unseen cord was even more substantial than the one holding us together. It was the most unforgettable experience of my life. Still, I didn't call what I felt unconditional love.

A tragic event that affected my extended family triggered my understanding of unconditional love three years after my son's birth.

On Friday, November 19, 1987, I returned home after working a ten-hour shift. I served dinner to my family, took care of my children, and began cleaning my house. Cleaning on Friday became a habit because I wanted to spend more time with my family on the weekend.

That Friday was no exception. I completed my chores, made myself a cup of tea, and sat on a couch to unwind. I loved watching the late news while sipping my drink. It was early in the morning when I turned the TV on to hear the breaking news. A shooting had happened at two o'clock in the morning in Brighton Beach, Brooklyn, New York, not far from where we lived. Russian Mafia shot a Russian immigrant in the back of his head while he sat behind the wheel.

As soon as I heard the announcement, I had a premonition. I immediately thought of a distant relative. Involuntarily, I heard myself say, "Oh, no! I hope it wasn't Aunt Rosa's son."

Aunt Rosa was related to me through my father's sister's marriage and was the daughter of my uncle's brother. We met once, briefly, when I was a teenager. It wasn't until I moved from Ukraine to Moldova in 1971 to attend a college that fate brought us together. Aunt Rosa was much older than me. She was married and had two sons.

During her stay, as we learned more about each other, we became close, and by the time Aunt Rosa left, we formed a bond. She invited me to visit her and her family in Lviv, Ukraine. It took me two years to get there.

On my visit, I met Boris, one of her sons. My aunt told me he was trouble, and at seventeen, he had a hard time staying in school because he defied authority. Boris was unruly and out of control.

I felt terrible for my aunt and couldn't understand why Boris acted that way. His life was a dream every kid in the USSR desired. Everything he needed was provided for him by his loving parents.

My stay was delightful. Aunt Rosa's apartment was on the second floor facing Gorky Park, named after the famous Russian writer Maxim Gorky. It was autumn, my favorite time of the year, and the night air was crisp. I slept with windows open and, in the morning, when I opened my eyes, a kaleidoscope of colors created by the fallen leaves greeted me.

I enjoyed visiting Gorky Park, a fairy tale place. In its magnificent environment, I saw majestic black swans swimming gracefully in the lake for the first time in my life. Their exquisite beauty forever captured my heart.

I spent two unforgettable weeks with my newfound family. Aunt Rosa treated me like a princess, and her husband, David, doted on me. Aunt Rosa, who always wanted to have a daughter, complimented my beauty and tucked me into bed each night. I was too glad to fulfill her void. Our goodbyes were sad, and I didn't know that many years would pass before I saw Aunt Rosa again.

I lost touch with Aunt Rosa when my husband and I immigrated to the United States of America. Mama joined us a year later, and one day she mentioned that our extended family had also left the Soviet Union for America. Occasionally, I thought about my aunt and wished to reconnect with her, but for some crazy reason, I couldn't recall her last name.

Thirteen years later, when the reporter mentioned the victim's name on that fateful evening, I remembered—and knew that my hunch had come through. I never imagined our next reunion would occur under such tragic circumstances.

As a mother, I ached for my aunt. I had a hard time understanding the cruelty of life because no parent should outlive their child. Sadly, it is not always the case.

Inside the darkened room, with the TV as its only illumination source, I stared at the screen and thought of Rosa. Petrified, I watched the gruesome picture of a man covered in blood and slumped in the driver's seat with his head on top of the steering wheel. The back door of the Nissan Maxima was open as if whoever sat behind had left in a hurry. The camera kept switching back and forth between the crime scene and the announcer, and I watched it alone with my tea forgotten. Dumbfounded, I sat there with tears streaming down my cheeks. My body shook so hard I heard my teeth rattle. I couldn't wrap my brain around what had just happened. *Why Rosa, of all people?*

I knew I needed to contact my aunt, but her number was unlisted when I searched the phone book. Discouraged and exhausted, I went to bed.

In the morning, I called Mama and asked her to buy a Russian newspaper, hoping I could find some helpful information. Boris' death made the front page, but no contact information existed on his family.

Out of desperation, I called the editor. Surprisingly, he gave me my aunt's phone number. Relieved, I dialed it, but upon hearing the troubled voice of a person who answered, I chickened out and hung up. Before I redialed, I took a while to compose myself. This time, I asked for Rosa, and when I heard her voice, I offered her my deepest condolences and arranged a visit.

When I rang the doorbell, her husband, David, opened the door. I hugged him and told him how sorry I was about his loss. He showed me to the living room, where I saw what remained of my Aunt Rosa. I couldn't find a trace of the beautiful woman I once knew and admired. In front of me was an empty shell of a human being.

I listened to Aunt Rosa's listless voice as she talked about her departed son. She recalled how good he was to his mama. Her son adored and showered her with love and affection. Aunt Rosa did the same in return despite him being imperfect. Her son broke her heart, but she continued to love him.

In Aunt Rosa's eyes, Boris was a good son.

It was then that I finally understood the true meaning behind the two simple words—*unconditional love*. It was then that I realized a mother's love is unconditional. An invisible umbilical cord connects the unconditional love between a mother and her child. This unseen thread is unbreakable until the mother takes her last breath.

Years later, whenever I hear a story of a child's imminent demise, I think of a mother whom I haven't met but whose sorrow and love for her child I grasp entirely. I know this love because it is the kind I call *unconditional*.

ETYA VASERMAN KRICHMAR

Etya Vaserman Krichmar was born in Kazakhstan, USSR. For twenty-three years, she experienced anti-Semitism, persecution, and discrimination. In 1977, claiming human rights violations, together with her spouse and two-year-old daughter, Etya sought asylum in the United States of America. Her family's request was granted, and on March 7, 1978, Etya took her first step in the land of the free.

Writing became Etya's passion and saved her life after she underwent massive brain surgery. During the prolonged recovery, she wrote *Living in Fear*, a memoir about her life under a totalitarian regime. Etya's opinion pieces were published in *TC Palm* newspaper, and her stories can be read in *White Rose* and *Write Launch* magazines, Reedsy, and Medium. In addition to creative writing, Etya enjoys gardening, needlepoint, and caring for her two miniature dachshunds. She is retired and lives in Port Saint Lucie, Florida, with her husband.

Erasing Childhood

Thierry Lagarde

Near Bordeaux, France, late 1957. Stranded a few weeks in the care of my father's mother in rural, postwar unsanitary conditions, I am confronted with consequences embedded deep down the core of my forming bones—femurs, shins, ankles, and knees—a structural path shattered as hips and spine curve to adapt. I entertain vague memories of defending myself from a camouflaged enemy. No images. Instead, exacerbated sensations of my endless fall to sabotage. The precocious child—I am no more. Foundations shattered, turmoil churns through tunnels of doubt, roaring to greet me in the face of denial. As an uninvited guest cheats at this poker game, my future is being gambled. I am twenty months old and just crossed swords with the virus poliomyelitis.

Endless forceful waves crash along the shores of my dignity. One childhood encounter, a lifetime shock. With little vocabulary to react, I surrender to submission and wait. Dice are rolled. Living up to consequences is the challenge.

౪

Now six, it's been four years since my family landed as immigrants in Canada. Living in New Brunswick, a young boy in hiding from his imperfections, I master my capacity to avoid adults from the household as I am kept away from normalcy. Time, backed by hope, appears to deal with reality as differences accentuating my unequal steps inevitably bloom. Walking, I manage. Crawling feels more like it.

This morning, lying on the sidewalk after a brutal fall, I look up to you, Mother, helpless. You stand, Mom, silent, eyes empty. Never has a moment in time felt so long in the hopes of a gesture. I smile, imploring. *Is it a plea to endless blue skies surrounding motherly love?* I question silently.

Motionless, you are waiting for me to get up.

My left foot lies distorted, inward. Calf muscles deny themselves expansion.

Don't you realize something is wrong in my capacity to grow and communicate? I question as I lay astonished. *Is there someone at the other end of the receiver?*

Unanswered, unexpressed questions lock me in.

With my brothers' help, I get up. Off to school we go as life ignores another signal of distress sent toward unlit lighthouses. Wrapped in silent foghorns surrounded by misty fogs, dying to myself, I crawl back into shame.

Home, my every move is scrutinized. I feel uneasy. I am incapacitated although I feel whole.

∞

For seven years now, I've disappeared for others, in hiding as the mean one who damaged his mother's projects of greatness. A once-upon-a-time-promising child, weighing down adults' deflated ambitions, punctuated by my deficiencies. Words of dismay trap my being, step by step, down the cellar of resignation.

Intrusive thoughts are now a familiar pattern. I obey and wander out of forceful thunderclouds to shine in my own darkness. Lying under covers of negation, I fray to sustain the flame, a murmur of a twinkle, invisible to others. When they would like me to appear for their façade, I am nowhere to be found. A behavior or reflex polished to perfection. By closeting me in such an undignified manner, you unwillingly offer me, in exchange, the power to say no to appearing before you or anyone in public. It is called shutting down. Counterfeit shyness. Crushed self-esteem. The ultimate excuse for the vivacious child not to show up.

I operate within these realms, unaware of the price I will pay later. Suffocating beneath the hand-sewn quilts of past family stories weighing down my unballasted spirits. Determined to free myself from this scenario's worst role. Living by others' needs, erasing my coming to life.

In defiance, I die every breath.

℘

In 1963, still lingering, I am unexpectedly taken eight hundred miles west to Montréal, part of a road trip in wonder. Subsequently, to my first major surgery. I wake up, a shining silver wire seeping from my tender left underfoot flesh, held in place by a four-hole button—until!

"Until what?" I can't recall. This procedure, which no one explained to me, is supposed to help me walk straight, eventually. *Oh, okay!* "Can we go to the pool?"

"No."

Torment buried, smiling, I accept my fate as a present—silver wire ribbons and all.

Estranged from pain, I am growing up. The tangible big black button is sown under my foot, securing displaced sinews to metal threads. *Fascinating,* I think. "Do I get to keep it?"

"No." Annick, my mother, faints.

℘

Sixteen, now living in Québec. Six long years since I left the villages of the Acadian Peninsula, leaving behind my soul for preservation. Life between my parents attains summits of disorder: Conflicts smash against the fortress of my youth as cups of fuming dark coffee catapult over my head during breakfast. Brooms pierce wooden doors, punctuate endless silences, clash against words of destruction. I built walls of unparalleled dimensions for the struggling repressed teenager I've become.

Surgery, to stop growth in my right leg to prevent further distancing of the left one, is performed. As evaluated by specialists, it will catch up by the time I'm twenty.

Last night, Annick—who does not want her five children to call her *Mom* or *Mother* or any word reminding her she gave birth—sent her typewriting machine down two flights of hardwood stairs. She refuses to type another word forced on her as my father's improvised secretary, claiming her own voice, shrieking.

I hold on, trembling, to unspoken defeats: When lies rule in the face of youth, broken on the backbone of trust. When a newborn's celebration runs alongside nightmares. Days spent dodging predators, towering in their insatiable hunger to divide and reign.

In control, Mom, you ensure the umbilical cord of suffering at a leash's length does not part from the prey. "Beware to not delve in waters other than from my womb."

I comply, ignorant.

As endless spider webs, Mom knits years of frustrations into locks of unexpressed, distorted emotions. Not a comma in building sentences for seventeen years—words extinct, fully exhaled in one breath—as I have entirely muted myself through high school.

Pain, stockpiled in mismatched bones, results from lying under the meaning of sentences. *Do you really want me to disappear? Mother? Father? Grandmothers?*

Again and again, smashing the need to explode from the crackling shell, I submit so you can shine. Somehow, the numerous scars you left adorning my warped, estranged soul are an open window to inner beauty: a force not yet expressed, alive and unalterable. *I put such empowering trust in you, Mom.* If a powerful virus could not floor me, clinging to survival within childhood determination, when you are gone—winds of songs fiercely running along dunes of words piling up, surrounding into crescendos of deep oceans protectively rocking me—I will come to life.

Poliomyelitis, P-O-L-I-O, the ultimate, forbidden five-letter contraction, certainly destroyed your ambitions, Mom. It assailed my body, my frail, coming-to-life envelope I manage to love to this day—in the face of your shame of me, shattering your idea of perfectionism, an altered state you never forgave me for accepting as my own.

Polio, like other viruses, has been my shelter growing up, as crooked as it might sound, becoming my win and guidance while eluding Dad's verbal violence at its peak, wrapped in jealousy toward us teenage boys. Your destructive actions, Mom, are no more needed for me to appear. Father's disregard of his children's needs, while endlessly completing his doctorate in linguistics, leaves me with no diploma as I quit high school at seventeen. Doubled by a proper understanding that I will never conceive children until I find myself.

And then it will be too late, another desire vanishing.

You, Mom—at this hour while you are enticing us teens, luring us toward your bodily attributes without success, sharing your stories about climaxing while breastfeeding as your idea of nurturing, your multiple vicious attempts at breaking down my spirits through bodily offenses—somber joy is taking over your ill senses, Mom, sharing sordid details of such encounters while caressing a flute of champagne.

I repeatedly dive to emerge. *Only when death do us part will I reunite the broken pieces.*

Today, at sixty-six, appearing as a golden *kintsugi* collage, a brilliant amalgam of precious keepsakes defining the essence never altered, respectfully being true to the flickering light of self, I reappear, laying words of my own illustration.

In your ending and my beginning, I have lost my mind; it is just as well. A state not owned, imposed, lapsed as I put your ashes in a fancy pottery urn adorned in seductive feminine dancers, your final golden cage, locked in a glass niche, enthroned in a high-end mausoleum on Mount Royal, downtown Montréal, a perfect bunker responding to your ideals of protection from a deranged world.

As acceptance—key to the nature of things—brings back to life shreds of my own mystified soul, freed from volatilized hurricanes, I will shine as my own.

THIERRY LAGARDE

Thierry Lagarde, born in Tours, France, spent his childhood and molded his soul on the Acadian Peninsula, off the shores of New Brunswick, Canada. Québec adopted him at ten, and Montréal was the city in which he spent his adult life. Thierry describes himself as being raised by three continents. His bustling life is in Montréal, Québec. He chose English, his second language, to express his love for communication through words.

Thierry, a natural caregiver, is passionate about people. He contributed a major part of his working career to enhancing the lives of many living with mental health challenges. Children and their struggles are at the center of his concern in writing. An artist at heart, Thierry gives free rein to his zeal for collecting eclectic artifacts of everyday life and transforming them into attractive, humble art objects. He is an accomplished jewelry craftsman as well as an avid gardener.

A Turning Point Message from God

Darlene Atkinson Lamb

For a number of years, I tried to heal our broken marriage. No progress had been made with any of our issues as I was the only one committed to trying. I spent close to forty years being blamed for things that didn't work the way my husband wanted them to. My last straw was when our youngest grandson at the time, Adam John Weber, age five and a half months, died on March 3, 1994. The doctors said it was SIDS. I felt so lost and alone in my grief, completely and emotionally broken.

One afternoon, about a month later, I lay on my bed in the darkened bedroom, feeling depression hovering near me. Hugging a pillow close to my heart, tears welled up again and sobs erupted. I began talking to a silent God, crying out my sorrows, my fears—expressing my heart and soul's grief. I pleaded to God for help. "I give up," I heard myself cry. "I can't do this by myself anymore." I lifted my arms and laid my sorrow and grief at God's feet.

The human part of me had given up, but my soul gave it *up*.

About a week later, a friend who was a registered massage therapist gifted me a massage. Afterward, while sharing a cup of tea, I noticed a deck of cards lying on the kitchen table. "What are these?" I asked curiously while picking them up.

"They're oracle cards. I choose one card each day for inspiration or guidance," she explained.

"Can I try?"

"Of course."

As instructed, I shuffled the cards, spread them out on the table, closed my eyes, and moved my hand over them, paying attention to my intuition. "Here . . ." I heard coming from within. I put my finger down, opened my eyes, picked up the card, and read:

"Now is the time for you to start looking at the cloud people for a message."

"Well, that's weird," I thought and went home.

∞

Victoria Day is celebrated on the weekend nearest to May 24 each year in the Commonwealth. This is the official beginning of spring in Canada, when the provincial parks are opened for the season, having been closed during the winter. Chris, a young fellow who had been living at our home for four years while attending university, invited me to spend a weekend before the opening of Killbear Provincial Park, up on Georgian Bay on Lake Huron. He worked many summers there studying the massasauga rattlesnakes. This seven-square-mile piece of land—with its rugged, rocky shoreline mixed with sand beaches and beautiful views of windswept pines on rocky islands—is known for its beautiful sunsets.

No visitors would be in the park except the young staff who were preparing for its opening the following weekend. I would stay in the staff house with everyone, and while they all had work to attend to, I would have the whole park to myself. I accepted the invitation and intended to spend my alone time communing with nature's springtime beauty by hiking and photographing.

I packed my suitcase with a few necessities, some food supplies, and my camera, a Minolta XL200, and on Friday afternoon, I drove three hours north toward my destination—and destiny.

I spent Saturday hiking and photographing the early signs of spring. I had never been in this beautiful park before, so I kept to the well-beaten paths through the forest. The weather was too cool for the snakes to have awakened from hibernating, and mosquitoes and black flies had not hatched, so my precious time was spent breathing in the fresh spring air, feeling the sun through my favorite lime-green hoodie, and finding flowers, birds, and landscapes to photograph. I was content to just follow myself around, taking in the peace and quiet of being alone with Mother Nature.

Chris and I had made plans for after supper, taking a hike to Harold's Point to watch the sunset. Everything went as planned. We arrived just in time and found a large iconic gneiss rock. This coarsely grained metamorphic rock had pushed up from deep within the earth and had alternating layers of gray and black feldspar, quartz, and sparkling bits of pink mica. It was a perfect height to become a place to sit. I sat down, turned to face the western sky, and saw the most beautiful cloud I had ever seen. It was in the shape of an angel carrying what looked like a baby in her outstretched arms, presenting it to the heavens.

With my heart in my throat, I leaned down and quickly took my camera out of its case, attached it to my tripod, turned it on, and tried to slow my breathing and thoughts. My heart was racing, checking all my manual choices: Remember to take off the lens cap. Stay calm. Compose the shot. Check. Breathe. Double-check. Make sure everything is in focus. Hold my breath. Push the button. Click. Look through the viewfinder again . . . Press down for one more shot. Done.

The Gift

The cloud had shifted.

Chris and I watched this cloud slowly drift north.

While we watched silently, I heard words inside my mind that told me, "No matter whatever happens in the world, everything IS okay."

I believe this was God's voice answering my prayer for help. The words didn't say everything will *be* okay but rather, everything *is* okay.

I have never forgotten these powerful words and remind myself of them often. They help me understand the hurtful and traumatic events of my life. I think about birthing myself alone while my mother was under anesthetics, how my father died when I was four and I was told he had "just gone away," the surrendering of my firstborn child for adoption, my sorry marriage, the abandonment of my husband and our three grown children, my growing old alone. These things were hard to understand—but now these words remind me over and over again that everything *is* okay. When I repeat these words, my body relaxes, my soul sighs, and I accept their reality.

Darlene Atkinson Lamb

Even though the atrocious and tragic happenings on earth—both past and present—make it difficult to believe that everything *is* okay, I try intensely hard to believe in my heart that it is.

I titled this image "The Gift" in honor of my grandson Adam, who died too early, but who lives on forever in the hearts of those who knew and loved him.

Seeing this angel cloud and hearing its message was a turning point for me in this lifetime. A turning point I look back at to see that life truly is a miracle.

DARLENE LAMB

Darlene Lamb is a late bloomer to writing. Her first passion was photography, but during the pandemic, she realized she needed a different project. Darlene pulled out her old journals, joined the online group of Life Writers (LifeWriters.us), and began writing her memoirs. This satisfied her need to be creative, and she discovered the writer/poet who lived inside her.

Darlene is an international photographer. Her work in England, Italy, Mexico, Cuba, and many places in North America can be found hanging in art galleries, corporate business offices, universities, hospitals, and health care offices, as well as in private homes.

Now, Darlene has found a new passion for writing, and while the story of the angel cloud has been written for newspapers and magazines by others, this is the first time it has been published in her own words.

Speak Louder

Eve M.

I've spent a great deal of my life holding my tongue. Ever agreeing, so as not to make anyone angry or upset with me. Afraid if I said what I really felt or thought, I would be unlovable. Left behind to blow away like a tumbleweed in a dust storm.

When I was a teenager, I wanted to run away from home. A boy I went to school with offered me refuge for a night. He snuck me into his room, careful not to alert his parents. A pungent smell of dirty socks filled the room; clothes and used food wrappers were strewn around the floor.

"You can lie in my bed," he said as the sky turned from crimson to dark gray.

I trusted him. He was a quiet boy; he always seemed harmless at school.

He lay next to me. I felt his hot breath on my neck. I closed my eyes and pretended I was asleep. As I lay there, I felt him moving toward me, pressing his body against my back. I took shallow breaths, careful not to move a muscle. I nearly jumped as I felt his sweaty hands move between my thighs. With one finger, he pulled my underwear to the side, inserting another inside me. I held my breath until he was done with me. I never said a word to him.

I figured, since I didn't speak up, I deserved it. Perhaps I owed him for giving me a place to stay.

A few years later, when I was seventeen, I kept silent in my marriage too. I married a man I thought I would spend forever with. A month into our marriage, he shoved me so hard—I flew in the air from one side of the room to the other and sprained my wrist breaking the fall.

"It's your fault for landing like that." He shouted at me as I tried to absorb the impact of what took place.

For several years, I watched as I become someone different. I became feeble, insecure, afraid. As the abuse continued to escalate, I began to isolate myself, hiding from family and friends. I'd curl into the fetal position as he pounded on my face with one hand and choked me with the other. I thought he would kill me, that one day his rage would overtake him, and he wouldn't stop until I was gone. I resigned to this being my fate.

Life was too painful and not worth living.

When I got pregnant, suddenly, there was this little guy I wanted to protect at all costs. Life didn't feel dark anymore. Brandon made me want to live just so I could hold him in my arms and see him smile.

My husband didn't allow me to work. Having a job would mean interacting with people—people I might tell about the abuse or men who might sweep me off my feet and steal me from him. I started daydreaming about how I would leave and where I would go when I did. I had to shield Brandon from this life.

I didn't know how I would take care of the two of us.

I spent all my time loving Brandon, and when I got a beating, it was easier afterward because I could hold my baby. When Brandon turned two, my husband allowed me to have a paper route. I would get up at three a.m. and put Brandon in the car with me as I drove around and slung papers out the window.

Every week when I cashed my checks, I kept five dollars out to stuff in a dresser drawer. It was the most I could save without my husband noticing. I was determined to give my son a better life. I didn't want him to be raised in this violent manner; I didn't want him to become the same.

When I got pregnant for the second time, I resigned to the idea of ever being free because I would never be able to care for two children on my own. I was a high school dropout with a GED and no job experience other than the restaurants I worked at before I became a prisoner.

Nine months later, Seth was born, another angel sent from heaven. These babies were sent to save me—there could be no other explanation.

When Seth was six weeks old, I came out into the living room after midnight to find my husband beating off to porn on the television. I didn't like porn, but the truth was, I would have used any excuse to leave. The next morning, I got up and packed a bag. I started shoving things in from the boys' bedroom: clothes, diapers, bottles, whatever I could grab.

"You're a piece of shit. I'm leaving you." This voice I didn't recognize was speaking up, demanding to be heard. A new strength pulsed through my veins. With the small black diaper bag slung over my shoulder, Brandon in one hand and Seth in the other, I made my way toward the front door.

My husband kneeled before me. "Please don't leave." Spit flew from his mouth, dribbling onto his chin.

I looked into his eyes and saw him for what he was: weak and pathetic.

I was no longer a tiny, afraid woman. I was a goddamn lioness, and no one could have stopped me that day.

"Get the fuck out of my way." The beastly woman who had been hiding in my soul took over.

"Please don't leave me. I love you. Don't leave. I'm sorry, I'm sorry, I'm sorry."

I felt satisfied as he groveled at my feet. For the first time, he was afraid.

"I am leaving, and these are mine," I said, lifting Brandon a little higher off my hip and then raising the infant carrier to display Seth.

My husband didn't move.

"Get the fuck out of my way!" The voice roared from the depths of my stomach. If I made a ruckus, he would eventually move. I knew he would fear that someone would call the cops, and he would have to pay for his crimes.

Holding tight to my boys, I reached down for whatever I could grab. I wrapped my fingers around a candlestick and chucked it at the window. It bounced back, landing on the carpet. I was a madwoman throwing whatever I could reach—a framed photo, a knickknack of a cat—defeated each time the object bounced back. Finally, I wrapped my fingers around the television remote and threw it like I was trying to earn a position on a pro baseball team, the boys never leaving my arms. The remote met the glass pane and shattered through it right out into the front yard.

My body tingled with satisfaction.

He moved aside, still begging.

I unlocked the door and walked away, this time for good. I finally stood up for myself. My boys saved me. They gave me a reason to want to live. And that is just what the three of us did. I have called upon the brave woman who lives within me several times throughout my life. I still have a hard time speaking up, but those are the times I remind myself that speaking up is always an option.

EVE M.

Eve M., who spent part of her life hiding, most of her life fighting, and all of her life loving completely, discovered her joy for writing when she was a teenager. Writing became an escape from an often-cruel world and the thing that kept her sane throughout life's challenges. Eve uses her love of the written word to figure out who she is, what it all means, and how to find her way out and continue moving forward when the world tilts beneath her feet.

Eve is currently working on her first memoir. Having lived a complex life, she has an abundance of insight, wisdom, and relatable stories to share with her readers.

Goodbye Dream, Hello Real World

Lou Martindale

"Grandma, may I please, please, puleeease play your piano?" I begged every time I visited my grandparents' home.

"Yes, for fifteen minutes," she usually answered.

Not wasting a minute, I ran to the piano, carefully raised the cover, and then, in an exaggerated Liberace-like manner, raised my hands and let them fall on the piano keys. My fingers flew up and down the keyboard, playing soft and loud, fast and slow, staccato and legato, making up the melody as I played. Occasionally, I jumped off the bench and performed a low bow to my imaginary audience seated in a great concert hall.

Growing up in Flint, Michigan, in the 1950s, I had a happy and carefree childhood. I was the oldest, with a sister four years younger and a brother six years younger than me. On the weekends and in the summer, we lived in a hundred-year-old log cabin on Lobdell Lake. Laughing and running through the woods, we played children's games. When wild blackberries and huckleberries were ripe, we picked buckets full of juicy berries, eating as we picked; the juice

Lou standing beside cabin
on Lobell Lake

ran down our faces and stained our fingers. We built fires to roast hot dogs and make s'mores and, at night, captured fireflies in Mason jars, trying, without success, to make lanterns. Almost every day, we swam in the lake and fished from the dock. I explored every nook and cranny of the medium-sized lake in my rowboat. Mother didn't drive a car, so around age twelve, I was allowed to take the motorboat to the grocery store across the lake when we needed groceries.

I loved to water-ski and pestered my dad every single day when he got home from work to take me skiing. He was tired from a long day of standing on a production line, but nevertheless, he agreed to take me. Neither of my siblings could water-ski, so it was just Dad and me out on the lake. I once swam all the way across the lake and back, a total distance of about two miles. Dad followed me in the rowboat just in case I needed help.

During inclement weather and at night, we read or played games. I loved to read and spent many hours curled up reading books checked out from the library in town. We didn't have a television or telephone. Why would we need them? We had the whole world to explore physically and through books.

More important to me than running through the woods, water-skiing, swimming, boating, fishing, and even reading was my love of playing the piano. I don't know what first attracted me to the piano. We didn't have one, and I never heard anyone play Grandma's piano. Beginning around age seven, I started begging for a piano. Finally, my dad bought a well-used player piano at auction and had it delivered to our basement. A damp basement is *not* a good place for a piano—not that it made any difference to this piano where it was placed. It was out of tune, the B key below middle C—along with other keys—didn't work, and the wood had been badly mistreated, but I didn't care. I had a piano.

And now that I had a piano, I begged for piano lessons, and after a short while, a teacher was found. I really don't know how my parents afforded my lessons. Weekly lessons cost five dollars per half hour. That is equivalent to about fifty-six dollars in 2022. My mother didn't work, and my dad worked on the production line at General Motors, Chevrolet Division. He had five people and two homes to support.

I loved playing the piano and never had to be reminded to practice. At some point, my teacher, Mrs. Alice Thayer, told my parents I had the potential to be a concert pianist. Was it a ploy to get them to continue my lessons? I don't think so because she entered me, at age eleven, in the annual National Guild of Piano Teachers competition, and I won first place that year and the next year. For eight years, I practiced diligently and played in recitals and competitions. I loved playing for an audience. I was on my way to becoming a concert pianist.

Gift from my grandparents—a new spinet piano

I had been taking lessons for five years when, in 1956, my grandparents bought my family a brand-new spinet piano. I did not have to play on an old, beat-up piano in the basement any longer. Our new piano stood upstairs in a place of honor in our living room. Finally, I had an in-tune piano, and all the keys worked. I was in heaven.

Life was so good. I had an exciting future ahead of me. Then, in September 1958, when I was sixteen—*boom!* My life took a drastic turn, and not for the better.

We moved from Flint to Albuquerque, New Mexico. Gone was my beloved cabin on the lake. Gone were my carefree summer days. Gone were my lifelong friends. And *gone* was my piano teacher.

After the move, I tried to find a new teacher. But after trying out several and discovering they couldn't help me toward my goal, I became discouraged. My high school choir director suggested inquiring at the University of New Mexico for a music professor who gave lessons. I did find a professor who would have been able to continue my training, but more times than not, he failed to show up at the agreed-upon lesson time.

Finally, in despair, I quit.

I quit trying to find a teacher. I quit playing the piano.

For the first time in its life, my piano sat in the corner—quiet, alone, and untouched.

With my dreams of being a concert pianist taken away, I felt there was nothing left in life for me. My life spiraled downward until I reached a nothingness existence. I didn't know anyone in this new town. The only water was the muddy and dangerous Rio Grande River. There were no woods to run in. Always an honor roll student, now my grades slipped to failing. I had no interest in anything—not school, not church, not family. Nothing. I didn't want to be in Albuquerque. I wanted to go home to Flint, live with my grandparents, and resume my previous life, but my parents would not agree to that.

I became a rebellious sixteen-year-old. If I couldn't continue with my dream of being a concert pianist, I was done with life. Feeling miserable, I made everyone around me miserable too. I rebelled against being forced to participate in family outings, which consisted only of going to church or visiting Native American pueblos. My parents seemed overly enthralled with the Native American culture, and we visited all the pueblos in our area.

On my birthday every year, we attended the Green Corn Dance on the Santo Domingo Pueblo. I didn't want to be there and resented that on my birthday, of all days, I was forced to do something I hated. To me, it was just a lot of drumbeating, with men dressed in ceremonial clothing and feathered headdresses chanting unintelligible words and jumping around on the hot, dry, bare desert dirt, causing a dust cloud to spread out and cover everything in the area—including me.

While I never got over the loss of my dream, eventually I adjusted, and my life went in another direction. I discovered boys, got married, and moved away from Albuquerque. We raised two daughters, watched them get married, and welcomed grandchildren. My life was happy and full again.

However, sometimes life has a way of letting you know that things happen for a reason. A few years ago, I was diagnosed with Dupuytren's contracture, a problem with the palms of my hands. The doctor advised avoiding certain activities that would aggravate the condition and could cause my hands to permanently curl inward. Playing the piano was one of the discouraged activities. What if I had followed my dream and my entire life up to that point had been dedicated to being a concert pianist? The diagnosis would have been the end of my career, leaving me with nothing to fall back on.

I'm not that rebellious sixteen-year-old girl now, and after seventy-nine years, I've matured and learned to embrace other things that fulfill and make me happy. Now, I get enjoyment out of just listening to classical piano music. Most days at my home, you can hear piano music playing softly in the background. Many happy events in my adult life, such as having a family, might not have happened if I had devoted myself solely to performing on a concert stage. My life has had its share of twists and turns. What was a turning point in my life in 1958, in the end, made me stronger to face those many twists and turns.

LOU MARTINDALE

Lou Martindale grew up in Michigan and moved several times before eventually settling in Brandon, Florida, in 1978. In 2018, she relocated to West Monroe, Louisiana. She is semiretired with over twenty-five years of experience as a technical writer, webmaster, and marketing specialist. In 2015, she graduated from the Bloomingdale Life Story Writing program in Brandon and was hooked. Her goal is to leave a written record for her descendants of what daily life was like for her from cradle to grave.

Before Lou began writing her own life story, she completed the biographies of her father, a World War II veteran, and her ninety-seven-year-old mother. She has been published in various publications. Lou enjoys gardening and reading, and she lives with her rescue cat, Lily Belle, who tries to *help* her write. Lou says, "Technical writing pays the bills, but creative nonfiction feeds my soul."

The Telegram

Stella Nahatis

At first, I thought I could talk him out of it. I stared out the window. Across the street, Mr. Norling was shoveling a snow-bank that had buried half of his car's tires. I kept my tears at bay when I turned to face my father. "We cannot move to Greece permanently. This is my home."

"You knew that from the time we brought you here. That after we had enough money we would move back."

My cheeks were burning, but I was still not crying. "You haven't talked about it for years, so I assumed we were staying here. Even after Mama died, you didn't say anything about it."

"You know that's why we bought the condominium in Thessaloniki."

"It's not fair. I'm an American, and I want to stay here."

A deluge erupted. I tasted the saltiness as I screamed for my rights and the unfairness of the move. "What am I going to do there? I thought you wanted me to become a teacher." The thought of that made my head feel like a cement block. I had wanted to go to a two-year college for just enough edu-cation to become a flight attendant. He insisted I become a teacher. I complied and was accepted at Boston State College.

"You won't have to work. Soon, you will get married and have a family."

I was certain Mrs. Paris upstairs could hear me, but I didn't care. "You are mean, taking me away after I am used to this lifestyle. I like going to Greece every summer, that's all. Not to live there forever."

By this time, he must have had enough. With his fists still clenched, my baba lowered his voice. "We are moving to Greece."

I didn't want to look at him anymore. I slammed my bedroom door and called Donna. Through my sobbing and sniffling, she got the message. Of course, she was shocked, but being from an immigrant family herself, she understood that we must do what our parents demanded of us.

A few days later, I approached the subject with my father. I persuaded him to let me stay one last summer in the United States. "You can leave after my graduation, but I should stay and spend time with my friends. And since you are planning for me to marry soon, I need to shop for my dowry. We should buy a trunk for all the household items."

His response without arguing surprised me. "Okay, in that case, you will have to travel by ship."

"You mean it, right? I can stay?"

Two weeks later, I relaxed when my baba announced, "I made my reservation for Greece. I will leave after you graduate. I asked Mr. Kutrubes, the travel agent, to find a companion for you with whom you can sail. He has a woman client who is planning a trip by ship in the fall. When she decides on a date, he will let you know to book a ticket with her. I don't want you to travel alone."

I flew all by myself when they adopted me at eleven years old. I did not speak a word of English, and now, at nineteen, he wants me to have a companion. I had come to terms with my moving back. I knew enough of the culture in which I was brought up. It was a good daughter's obligation to take care of her parents.

I pondered over my change of heart from eight years ago. Steve and Marianthe Pardalis had adopted me after my parents' fatal motorcycle accident. Eight years earlier, I had cried, begged, and prayed in silence to return to Greece. I could not stand being away from everything familiar. I couldn't stand the language barrier. It took me the entire school year to—somewhat—acclimate to my new country. But once I survived the excruciating adjustment period, I melded into the new culture to the point of no return.

But there I was, answering the call of another culture to fulfill the family obligation. I thought of the irony that my parents adopted an older child to have someone to look after them in their old age. The adult conversations I had overheard in Greece spoke about the pleasures and benefits of having children. Invariably, someone interjected, "That's why people adopt children, so they have someone to care for them in their old age." I took that to heart when I was adopted.

Both parents got a small taste of that benefit. I took care of my mother for two years during her bout with cancer, and then for three years, I managed the household duties for my father and me.

My father flew back to the old country, and I moved in with my cousin Veta and her family in Allston, a Boston neighborhood next to Brighton. Although Veta was a mere three years older than me, she had two adorable little girls. After two pregnancies, her medium height was proportionately complemented by the slender figure she maintained. I admired her neat appearance and impeccable grooming. Her short brown hair was in place whether she was at the kitchen sink, over the stove creating a delicious chicken soup, or bathing one of her toddlers.

On a quiet September day, I was on the floor with Mary, Veta's older daughter. Veta had shut the front door behind the young man in uniform. Mary was intently listening to me reading "Little Red Riding Hood." Her legs hung over one on each side of my thigh. She ran her pudgy little fingers across the page.

"What can it be?" Veta stood above us with the brown envelope.

Telegrams always piqued our interest and put us on alert. Our minds went to the worst possible scenarios: either a serious illness or death. It's not as though we never received telegrams to congratulate or announce a birth or a wedding, but for some reason, we always thought of the negative.

"Stella, he died, he died." Veta burst into tears.

I put Mary down on the rug. "Who died?" I snatched the piece of paper from Veta's hand.

"With sorrow we inform you your father died yesterday after suffering a heart attack. We buried him today."

The telegram was addressed to me.

Tears rolled down my cheeks. Mary got upset, watching us crying, and whimpered. She stretched her arms to her mother. It was a few minutes of crying and confusion.

I realized I was crying because Veta was crying. I didn't feel like I thought I should be feeling. After all, my father died. *Shouldn't I be feeling distraught? Truly sad? Shouldn't I feel sorry I was not with him?* But I did not feel the loss.

I think Veta was crying because that is what we knew people did when someone died. We hugged each other before she picked up Mary. I reread the telegram—and it dawned on me: *I don't have to move back to Greece. I can pursue my dream.*

I felt a tremendous sense of relief. I tried to suppress the excitement that thought aroused in me. Not that I felt guilty, but according to my cultural beliefs, I was supposed to drown in sorrow and be in deep mourning for the loss of my father.

Instead, I felt unabashed freedom.

Is it possible that by the age of nineteen I had developed an understanding of separation and death? Did I possess, at an early age, what it takes to overcome adversity without hysterics and melodrama? Was I born with that ability? In addition to the deaths of my parents, I endured the separation from my sister, who had been adopted by a couple in Greece; my beloved *theo* (uncle), my biological mother's brother; other relatives; my friends; and my country. Perhaps the combination of all these losses at a young age fortified me to accept setbacks and not fall apart.

Was I blessed with the belief that the spirit and the soul of loved ones live on and are close by when we need them? I know it is what I believe as an adult. With each challenge I faced, I accepted it and moved on. I admit I lost some of that easy acceptance when I faced challenges later in my life.

Not moving to Greece was not the only revelation to hit me: I could pursue my dream job. A seed must have been planted, unconsciously, in my eleven-year-old mind on board my first airplane flight on TWA. During my high school years, a searing desire to be a flight attendant was my constant companion. Following my father's death, I remained in the USA. I fulfilled my dream of becoming a TWA flight attendant—just like the lovely ladies on my first flight from Greece to my new country, America.

STELLA NAHATIS

Stella Nahatis was born in Northern Greece and lived there until her eleventh birthday. Adoption landed the eleven-year-old orphan in the United States of America. After overcoming the hurdles inherent to an immigrant, such as cultural differences, the language barrier, and assimilation, a strong and resilient Stella embraced her new country with fervor. Her passion and love for family, and people in general, have steered her into volunteerism beginning as a teenager. She embarked on a successful career with Trans World Airlines In-Flight Services.

Stella enjoys traveling, cooking, decorating for the holidays, and volunteering. She is most happy when surrounded by family and friends—whether at home, at a restaurant, at a dance, or on the golf course. Stella and her husband live in Manchester-by-the-Sea, Massachusetts. For additional information about Stella, go to StellaNahatis.com.

Seven or Seventy-Seven:
It's Still Puppy Love
Susan D. Owens

The Christmas I was seven, our tree was a work of art. A balsam fir that brushed the ten-foot ceiling in our living room, its evenly spaced branches extended a woodsy welcome of near-perfect symmetry. Dad always said he knew how to find the best tree on the lot; what he failed to dwell on (when we weren't teasing him about it) were his annual efforts to improve upon nature. By drilling holes in the trunk of his chosen selection and inserting branches from a supplemental *donor* balsam, he surgically altered each year's *au naturel* specimen to resemble the faultlessly shaped tree of his dreams.

Next came strings of multicolored bulbs backed by metal reflectors of contrasting hues. Treasured ornaments nestled among the branches, framed by individual strands of tinsel in strategic locations (tinsel symmetry being another of my engineer father's idiosyncrasies). Crowned by a flickering star, Dad's manufactured fantasy was the focal point of our holiday festivities.

On Christmas morning, waves of presents extended from the base of the tree to the middle of the room. Wrapping paper crackled as we opened our gifts with squeals of glee. Tantalizing smells from the kitchen promised breakfast delights. My parents' cigarette smoke spiraled upward in an era when smoking was neither recognized as a health hazard nor worthy of political commentary.

Outside, Mother Nature etched our windowpanes with ice-patterned art. Inside, frothy white snowflakes and Santas, stenciled with Glass Wax in childlike precision, offered worthy competition. Cold and snow were unremarkable for a Pennsylvania winter, especially in the 1950s, and the blaze of a log fire kept the chill out and the warmth in. In short, it was a perfect day.

And then it became more perfect. Dad, momentarily disappearing into the basement, emerged with a bundle wrapped in a towel. Only a tiny black nose, peeking from one corner, hinted at the surprise. "Looks like Santa left one more gift," said my folks, as my brother Steve, sister Chris, and I scooped up the tail-wagging ball of fluff, an eight-week-old, sable-colored collie. A miniature Lassie, his fur was soft as down, his tongue wet and insistent as he covered our faces with kisses, his puppy breath a vivid olfactory memory more than seven decades later.

Susan, Chris, and Steve with Prince, fall 1953

Susan D. Owens

We named him Prince, and for years he was our devoted sidekick, sleeping at the foot of our beds, never leaving our sides if we were sick, and chasing sticks in the yard. He died at the side of the road in front of our house the summer I was eighteen—hit by a woman in a hurry who didn't even slow down. That Christmas, the lights were a little dimmer, the celebrations a little more muted. Even the tree seemed a bit askew, though we were careful not to mention it to Dad.

Prince was the first of many canine companions, furry bodies over the years whose love and enthusiasm enhanced our joys and soothed our sorrows. The most recent one, a challenging mixed breed named Dex, left us in 2009. Afterward, my husband David and I agreed. *No more.* The anguish of parting was too painful, the responsibilities of starting again more than we were prepared to assume.

In 2010, we bought a motorhome and toured the country. In 2014, we moved to a one-story home more suited to our senior-citizen physiques. We relished the freedom and spontaneity of day trips without the worry of a pet at home. We welcomed unexpected guests without having to check the sofa for dog hair. We congratulated ourselves on making fiscally sound, logistically practical choices.

When the pandemic descended in 2020, pet adoptions soared. Starved for a diversity of human interaction, hundreds of thousands of households added four-footed companions. David and I added streaming channels.

We didn't want a dog. And we didn't have a dog, at least until the spring of 2022. Carol, a friend of a friend, was facing major surgery and needed someone to keep her pet while she recovered. A cute goldendoodle pup named Ollie, he'd been about the size of a teddy bear when we first met him.

We didn't know Carol well, but we still weren't traveling, and we had a fenced yard. Surely, we could be this little guy's foster parents for a few weeks.

I was seventy-seven when the pup arrived. Ollie was barely nine months. At fifty pounds, he was already as tall as the dining room table—more polar bear than teddy bear—but he extended his oversized love to all and accepted his new surroundings without a fuss. He also turned our lives upside down. Dog toys covered the living room floor. A giant dog bed took up residence in front of the filing cabinet in my office. David added *yard patrol* to his routine, ensuring his cleanup efforts included last-minute reconnaissance ahead of the lawn service.

We thought the dog would be with us for a couple of weeks. Two weeks turned into seven. With Carol's permission, we had him groomed, microchipped, and neutered. We bought treats, took him with us to garage sales, and tried hard to maintain the discipline of his excellent training: No feeding from the table. No getting on the bed. No jumping on anyone or anything.

All the while, he continued to grow. And dash around the yard in wild abandon. And wiggle his way into our lives. Carol was getting better, but her doctors cautioned against the dangers of caring for such a large dog. Seven weeks was rescheduled for thirteen. David and I found ourselves talking about "what if?"

"He's soooo cute," I said, "but for years we've said we didn't want a dog."

"Agreed," said David, "and in any case, we can't afford a dog. What if he gets sick?"

"And the vet bills become astronomical. We've been down that road before."

"I remember," said David, scratching Ollie behind the ears. "And even if he stays healthy, if he lives a normal dog's life . . ."

"We'll be in our nineties. And before we *get* to our nineties, I'd like to travel again. Who would watch him then?"

"I don't know," David sighed, handing Ollie a treat. "Besides, I thought we didn't want a dog."

"Absolutely. We're on the same page. No more pets."

We weren't the only ones talking. "I know you're worried about costs," my daughter said after a visit, "but if you have a chance to keep the dog, you should take him. I'll pay to maintain him."

Friends chimed in as well. "If you end up keeping that dog and you ever need to go somewhere, we'll be happy to babysit," said not one, not two, but three different families. We were sincerely touched by these generous offers, but we still didn't want a dog.

Ollie, impervious to ongoing discussions of his possible fate, continued to love us and everyone else he encountered. Like Prince, the collie of my childhood, he was our shadow, following us from room to room, giving us sloppy puppy kisses, rolling over for a tummy rub, watching doggie TV, and jumping with joy at the antics of his digital counterparts.

The day for Carol to reclaim her pet drew near. "I know we don't want a dog," I said, as Ollie looked up at us with honey-colored eyes, "but what if she can't take him back?"

"Then we'll just have to keep him," replied David with a grin. "What else can we do?"

Carol called three days later. "I've been giving it a lot of thought," she said. "I really love the dog, but I can't risk my health, so I'd like to give him to you. Is that okay?"

"Yes," I said, "that is more than okay."

It's been only a few months since Ollie came to us, but it's hard to remember what life was like without him. Freed from the constraints of maintaining discipline for someone else's pet, we now know that he likes blueberries and peaches and arugula and pistachio nuts. And that he can jump on the bed so quietly we don't even notice. And that the only thing he thinks is more fun than digging a hole in the backyard is having his muddy paws washed afterward in our shower.

"We didn't want a dog," David says frequently, "but I guess we needed a dog."

Perhaps we did.

Ollie, fall 2021

Ollie, fall 2022

We can't know what the future will bring, but we do know that our Christmas tree this year will stand a little straighter—even though it's artificial—and the lights will burn a little brighter because of the unexpected gift who has taken his place in our home and our hearts.

SUSAN DOUTHWAITE OWENS

Susan Douthwaite Owens, a native of Pittsburgh, Pennsylvania, began her first career as a technical publications manager for Westinghouse Electric. In 1982, she embarked on a second as the owner of Word Systems Associates, an IT consulting firm where she spent the next twenty years growing up with the industry.

Widowed after thirty-seven years of marriage to Dan Owens, Susan moved to Lexington, Kentucky, in 2003. Here she started a third career as a personal historian, helping individuals and families capture and preserve their stories in book form. She plans to change gears once more by the close of 2023, this time focusing fully on her own writing, including several memoirs and a series of family histories spanning ten generations.

Susan lives in Lexington with her delightfully unpredictable second husband, David Wilkes, their newly acquired goldendoodle, Ollie, and a lifetime of beautiful memories.

The Frazzled Farm Wife

Linda Monnahan Peterson

The biggest turning point in my life, I believe, happened after I moved to the farm following our marriage.

I was raised in a house of females; my frail, widowed mother, Ellen, and two younger sisters, Randi and Denise. On the periphery were five older married sisters and their families.

Mom and we girls lived in Gordonsville, a small town just inside the Minnesota/Iowa border, where my deceased dad had established and run Monnahan's Sawmill.

My work experience up to that point had been babysitting and, of late, working as a nursing assistant.

Despite the fact that our little burg was surrounded by agriculture, my exposure to farming was limited to visiting my sister Rosie and brother-in-law, as well as short trips to friends just out of town to buy eggs. Both families were dairy farmers.

Gordon, my dark-haired, hazel-eyed future husband, a farmer, came into my life as the result of a blind date arranged by my younger sister and her boyfriend.

At Gordon's friend's urging, Gordon wasted no time showing me his farm. This happened in the dark on our first date. My only thoughts about it at the time were, it was *way* out in the boonies—with the nearest neighbor a quarter mile away—and, if it was his farm, why were lights on in the house as we passed by?

I was later to learn that the preceding spring, Gordon had put earnest money on the 120 acres. He would take possession the following spring.

As they say, it was love at first sight. We were married just short of six months after that night. As I put the final touches on our wedding, alone at the church, I felt compelled to kneel at the altar, asking God to bless our marriage. Only he knew how much we would need it.

That spring, I became a farm wife. I had a lot to learn. My education in my new role began a few days either before or after the wedding, when Gordon presented me with a frozen, brown paper–wrapped package, saying, "This needs to be rendered."

Not having a clue what he was talking about, I opened the package to find masses of squiggly-looking, speckled pieces of pork fat.

These, he explained, needed to be fried at a low temperature so as to not burn the cracklings. The resulting product was to be strained to produce clean lard for frying or cooking. He neglected to tell me a greasy film would result from this process, landing on anything it touched, including our newly painted kitchen walls and cupboards.

Then, there were the in-laws. Two days after our wedding, Gordon's much older bachelor brother, with whom he farmed, appeared at our kitchen door just as we finished breakfast. Although it was planting season, and he was probably justified in this instance, this was to become a forty-plus-year pattern: Arnold, here, first thing in the morning, looking for a cup of coffee and some goodies. Usually, he'd reappear in the afternoon for the same reason, sometimes with their mother in tow.

Linda (first row, far right) and Gordon (second row, far right) in the tribe

If we were not up for the day when Arnold arrived, he'd scratch on our bedroom screen or, later still, drive the lawn-mower around the house until we unlocked the door.

Many members of the guys' large family followed suit, dropping in mostly without notice. Our house, it seemed, had a revolving door.

My next challenge was learning to chase, sort, and load hogs with these two. I should have been wiser when, one evening, Gordon *invited* me to participate in this practice by saying, "Don't plan anything in the house tomorrow morning. The hog trucker is coming at nine." That was shorthand for "We'll have to be up at six thirty to have those critters sorted and ready to go."

We were up with the sunrise the next morning, donning our most ragged, not quite clean jeans and knee-high boots, proper attire to wade through the muck of the hog yard.

I nearly gagged as the ammonia/rotten egg aroma wafted when we entered the yard.

One of the guys handed me a gate, measuring probably two-by-six feet, telling me to stand "over there" and pointing to a distant corner.

Yet, when I did just that, and some pigs were chased in my direction, the muck flew in every direction, including on my clothes and in my hair. *Auugh!* Then both men yelled at me for not stopping the one they wanted.

Was this man-turned-ogre in the hog pen *really* the quiet, shy guy who had wooed me just a short while ago? My mother had warned me, "Still waters run deep."

This scene was repeated many times that morning before I realized I was expected to run through the muck to attempt to stop a hog coming at me. I was a slow learner, but sooner or later, I caught on.

Soon, the trucker was pulling into the driveway. As he backed up to the loading chute, some of the hogs decided they weren't going to participate in this last ride. They turned around in the chute, heading back to the pen. When we finally got the last one on the truck, I asked the guys, "What do you want for breakfast? *Bacon* and eggs?"

We also raised and dressed (a misnomer to my way of thinking) broiler chickens. How you can call dunking a beheaded chicken into boiling water, stripping it of its feathers, and gutting it *dressing* is beyond me. But we did it for more than a couple of years.

One year, we raised five hundred of them, to be dressed here on

Linda and Gordon live the chicken experience

the farm by buying relatives. Many pots of water were boiled on our kitchen range. Piles of feathers and bird entrails littered the yard. Not a pretty sight.

A little less successfully, I learned to work with cattle. I loved working with the barn calves, teaching them to drink from a pail. Shoving their noses into the warm milk replacer, which I had mixed up while trying to rid it of its lumps. Seeing the look of surprise in their eyes when they discovered it was what they were after all along—and it tasted *good*!

I was not so successful working with the milk cows, what with the trouble of getting them into the barn and stanchioned, not to mention my battle with the milker.

I also learned to drop what I was doing when Gordon let out a blood-curdling yell, signaling his need of me to help hitch up a load. I eventually tired of this, telling him, "If you yell like that again, you'd better be caught in an auger!" (Watch those spring-loaded hitches—they almost cost me a finger.) And just know, while giving backing up directions, *you're* the one who's wrong.

I learned to drive a tractor when manpower in the field was short. On my maiden trip, four-year-old Chris rode with me. When I dropped the clutch too hard, he said, "Let me out! I don't ride with anybody who does wheelies in a tractor!"

When Arnold bowed out of pork production, I stepped in to help grind feed and muck out stalls.

Another of my adventures was learning to do farm bookwork and taxes. I did this not only for us but for Arnold as well. January became known as *tax fight time* since the guys challenged every figure I produced. They got their comeuppance when, much later, we hired an accountant to do our tax work. He commended me for a job well done.

Linda and Gordon with daughter Michelle and son Chris, circa 1980

Meanwhile, the kids were growing up, taking part in piano lessons and 4-H, where they did quite well.

While learning to do these things, you might ask, why didn't I just throw in the towel and say enough is enough? I may not always do it right, but quitting is not in my DNA. I come from a lengthy line of no-quitters.

I got my revenge by humorously recounting my farm adventures in a local newspaper column, "The Frazzled Farm Wife."

Much too late, I learned women raised in the rural environment are smart enough to not learn how to do everything. I was a town girl, more than willing to prove her worth as a farm wife. Besides, despite everything, I had come to love the country life—and had loved the farmer from the start.

LINDA MONNAHAN PETERSON

Linda Monnahan Peterson has been writing since being given a toy printing press and discovering poetry in grade school. She compiled a book of poetry for her classmates. In early adulthood, she took a writing course titled "Writing for Children and Teenagers," and she wrote a column, "The Frazzled Farm Wife," for the local newspaper. One of these stories, "The Hog Sorting Blues," made it into *National Hog Farmer,* the industry's premier trade magazine, and prompted fan mail from near and far.

Linda also contacted Erma Bombeck, telling her she intended to be the rural Erma Bombeck, to which Erma replied, "God love you. There should be more of you. I'll move over for anyone who can make the world less grim."

These days, Linda spends her time working on her memoir with the working title "Never Discount Spunk."

Dance Steps on the Sea

Jackie Raymond

My life drastically changed when, on April 18, 2002, my seventy-year-old beloved husband, Norman, died of pulmonary fibrosis at Orlando Regional Hospital. Only two of my five children were with me. Darby, Dawn, and Billy had already left. Bobby, Dianne, and I clung to one another in the hospital room as we sang along with "You Will Never Walk Alone."

Jackie and her husband Norman

Little did I know then that the lyrics of this song would apply not only to my husband's ultimate demise but to me as well. After forty-seven years of marriage, bereft of the love of my life, I became a widow.

How do I go on? My two miniature white poodles, Sebastian and Yvonne, provided comfort, and their required attention prompted me to live. But more than that, I know my unwavering belief in God helped me overcome the darkest moments of my life when I walked alone. With his help, I became a survivor. Ten years after Norman's death, I was strong enough to dance with the stars on an open-top deck of a cruise ship.

Thank you, God, for carrying me through.

Five months before Norm's death, our family went through the tragedy of Ryan's; our oldest, seven-year-old grandson burned to death in an automobile accident in south Texas. His death continued to haunt us, and Norm became bleaker in his poor physical state and frequently alluded to wanting to join Ryan to care for him in heaven. I believe this event expedited Norm's early death.

On March 23, 2002, at 4:30 a.m., I rushed Norm to the hospital. It was the Saturday before Palm Sunday, Universal's busiest time of year. I tended to my husband's hospital needs, cared for the puppies' well-being, and lived through the nightmare of running three businesses at the busy Universal City Walk in Orlando—alone.

As a teacher, I had no clue how to operate in a man-dominated business world. It was too much to deal with and overwhelming. Still, I put on Norman's shoes and took on his role of dealing with the Universal officials, along with my role of supervising the daily cart businesses.

These businesses came about in 1997 when Universal Studios in California officials asked our daughter Darby to open a duplicate open-type cart at the new Universal City Walk in Orlando, Florida.

Norm and I were semiretired at the time, but to help Darby, we agreed to run the operation in Orlando for her. Thus, our partnership evolved, and in 1999, we moved from St. Simons Island, Georgia, to Orlando.

With Norm gone, I had to carry on the legacy alone. My faith carried me through. Walk alone, stand up straight, or fall. *Thank you, God, for watching over me until I could walk.*

I could've fallen apart were it not for my Pilates classes. They were my salvation. I even went to a couple of spiritual massages. Halfway through one of them, an unreal experience occurred. I saw a vision of my deceased grandson upon a treadmill, reaching with one hand for overhead balloons and the other hand stretching behind me while calling, "Come, Papa,"—his name for Norman—"get the balloons with me."

God was letting me know both were happy in heaven.

The businesses at Universal flourished. We added a fourth cart, this time inside the new Islands of Adventure Park there. I managed all the cart business transactions on my computer, made the deposits, and worked different shifts at the carts. Darby placed my orders. Alex, my manager, oversaw the personnel, scheduling, and restocking of merchandise shipped to my house.

A year passed. Boredom and low-line depression loomed over me. Then, by the grace of God, a couple of things happened.

Ballroom dancing events began appearing on television. Occasionally, when the waltz and swing appeared, I stood and started dancing. Excitedly, my dogs jumped from their chairs and began barking and running in circles.

Then, I noticed an advertisement for dance lessons. From age seven, dancing was a part of my life. My parents were waltz competitors; by ten, my father had taught me to jitterbug, and I became his jitterbug partner. Now, I wandered in one day and signed up for several free classes. To my surprise, I was not as rusty as expected. The lessons were quite expensive. However, at the studio, I learned about dance cruise groups. On cruises, they had excellent dance teachers who taught two to four hours of lessons daily. In the evenings, there was open dancing. The ship's band played, and the group's teachers became the dance partners. I could go on three, maybe four cruises for what the studio's twenty classes cost.

On October 8, 2003, I sailed and danced aboard my first cruise—New York to Montreal, Canada—with the Merry Widows. I discovered other cruise dance groups, and I danced on ships sailing the Caribbean and Mediterranean Seas for eleven years.

My most memorable cruise occurred in February 2013, when I joined the Stardust Dance Company's group that sailed from Fort Lauderdale on the Italian *Costa Mediterranean* cruise ship. Its interior ancient Roman columns and décor were stupendous, but the bulkiness of this design caused the dance floor inside to be small. Thus, dancing was quite crowded. On the third evening, fellow dancers beckoned me to follow them to the top deck.

Exiting the elevator, I discovered another of the ship's fabulous design treasures. I saw a large oval-shaped wooden dance floor as I walked toward the host area. Everything was dark except the full yellow moon sending its shimmering glow upon it. The rooftop of the top deck was pulled back, which allowed us to see the vast black sky with millions of sparkling, diamond-like stars twinkling around the gorgeous moon. The incredible sound of the calm ocean lapping at the ship's side provided a melodic background to the music of the songs played on the host's CD player. Only two couples danced on the large dance floor. *What a joy! I won't be bumped or knocked off-balance.*

Glenn Miller's "In the Mood" began playing as we approached.

I tapped my feet and swayed my arms rhythmically. *Oops! I'll show my age. I was ten years old when I did the swing.*

Before I realized what was happening, one of the hosts grabbed my hand, and we began swing-dancing atop a ship. Ocean air tossed my hair this and that way, filling my nostrils with the fabulous salty ocean air. It soothingly caressed my face and body. My ears tingled with euphoric sensations.

As the song ended, the host escorted me to a seat to rest. We exchanged complimentary comments. Sitting, I soaked in the smell and taste of the salt air, the soft whirl of the breeze, enjoying the marvelous sounds around me.

Then, to my utter amazement, the "Tennessee Waltz" began to play. *My parents' favorite waltz song. I so wish they were here.*

An older host motioned for me to dance. We introduced ourselves as we walked to the dance floor. As instructed so many years ago by my parents, I raised my arms and elbows, placed my left hand on his upper right arm, extended my right arm out, and put my right hand on his left hand. After that, I lifted and tilted my head upward and turned it to the left. Coming up on the front part of my feet, I began to dance. The slight movements of my partner's hand on my back made it easy for me to follow. It was the magical moment I'd trained for over so many years.

As I glanced across the dance floor, I saw two lone, faintly seen bodies glide as one in perfect waltz form to the beautiful sounds engulfing them. *Oh my goodness!* It was my father in black pants, a black jacket, and a stiff white dress shirt, my mother in a shimmering, long-waisted, flowered silk ankle-length dress of the 1920s, dancing opposite us on the dance floor.

My white gauze ankle-length chiffon dress flowed sound-lessly in a ghostlike manner as my partner and I drifted effort-lessly around the entire span of the oval floor. The other lone couple seemed to float opposite us. The gentle rolling of the ocean waves created the perfect background rhythm to the "Tennessee Waltz." The dancing of the lights of the stars added an unreal backdrop.

As the music ended, I uttered, "Thank you. That was one of the most beautiful dances I have ever encountered. I shall always remember this as my most meaningful dance experience."

Looking around for the other couple, I saw them, ghost-like, slowly ascending upward into the star-studded night. At that particular moment, I thought, *Thank you, God, for carrying me after Norman's death until I was strong enough to walk and dance beside you.*

JACQUELINE "JACKIE" RAYMOND

This is Jacqueline "Jackie" Raymond's first publication. Her philosophy is, *Anything the mind Conceives can be Achieved if you Believe—CAB.*

Jackie was born in the 1930s in Cincinnati, Ohio. At age sixteen, her family relocated to warm Miami, Florida. She graduated from the University of Miami.

She married Norman Raymond and eventually moved to St. Simons Island, Georgia. They had five children, two boys and three girls.

Jackie, at age thirty-seven, received an MA in elementary education and taught for thirty years in Georgia and Texas.

In 1999, Jackie and Norman opened jewelry businesses at Universal Studios Orlando. Norman died in 2002, leaving Jackie alone to operate their business. Jackie joined a widows' group that went on ballroom dancing cruises; thus, this published story evolved.

During the COVID-19 lockdown, in 2020, Jackie joined Life Writers, unclogged her pen, and began writing her eighty-plus years of memoirs.

Pat

John Roche

I've been a maverick most of my life. As a child, I somehow loved skirting the rules. When I grew up, I tested authority every chance I could get. Never a good student, I don't know how many times my mother received letters from teachers saying, "John has ability. He just won't apply it." This boy barely squeaked through high school and flunked out of Wagner College on Staten Island as a freshman with a 0.62 grade point average (a D minus) a year later.

After my raucous freshman year in college, I enlisted in the United States Air Force. During my four active years in the service, I took classes that were made available to the military through several universities. By studying one course at a time, I raised my grade average considerably. After I was discharged from the air force in 1970, I returned to Wagner and graduated in 1973. To be honest, though, I didn't take the hardest route to a diploma. I took relatively easy courses: art, earth sciences, soft math classes, personal health, and various physical education offerings. My toughest course was German, where my standard answer became *"ein Glas Bier"* (German for "a glass of beer"). I just didn't get it. But the professor gave me decent grades for my effort.

Another class was Tennis 101 (and 102, 103, 104, ad nauseum). Lord knows that I fattened up my credit load with tennis. I wasn't a very talented player, but I enjoyed playing. It was where I met a wonderful instructor, Pat, who was not only a dedicated and talented educator but also a wonderful person. She embraced each student and took the time to ensure our success. There was no clock in her classroom. For the first time, I was learning, not rebelling against the authority figure.

I've never seen a warmer smile than Pat's. She looked at her pupils as real people, not just students. I can thank her for giving me accountability and inner comfort. Her favorite saying was "Peace." She meant it.

Periodically, Pat hosted gatherings for her students at her home, which overlooked the New York harbor. She took great pride in the fact that she wanted her home to be comfortable, so much so that many of us often fell asleep in front of the fireplace. That's how relaxed she made us feel.

Pat and I have kept in touch for the last fifty years. After I moved to Pittsburgh in 1974, I became a Pittsburgh Penguins fan. Pat has continued to root for the New York Rangers. It has given us a friendly rivalry and an introduction to our emails. Every time we chatted, there seemed to be little distance between us. We hadn't seen each other in thirty years until September 1, 2022, when my wife, Peggy, went to attend the US Open with my daughter, Morgan.

I tagged along to attend to some business of my own, most importantly to see my 102-year-old mother. I hadn't seen my mother for two and a half years due to COVID-19. We had a wonderful weekend planned. Friday, however, was Pat's day. I left Morgan's apartment in Astoria, Queens, where I hopped on the W train to South Ferry at The Battery in Manhattan. I could have taken an express, but I really enjoyed the people-watching on the local.

When the train reached the last stop, I raced up the stairs and noticed the modern ferry terminal that replaced the dingy building of old. I barely made the 11:30 a.m. boat and promptly called Pat to tell her I was on my way. She told me to look for her green Jeep at the pickup lot.

The ride over refreshed me. There's nothing like the New York harbor. All the boat and ship traffic is invigorating. Sailing past the Statue of Liberty gave me goosebumps.

At 11:58, the ship docked at St. George, and I went down the stairs to the pickup lot. There it was—the first car in line was a green Jeep. As I approached the SUV, five people jumped out of the car and headed for the terminal. *Oops! I don't think that's the right Jeep.*

A few minutes later, another green Jeep pulled up, and when Pat emerged, we hugged for what seemed like forever.

As Pat cruised Staten Island looking for a place to have lunch, I was impressed with the advancements that had taken place on *The Island* since I left forty-eight years ago. Adjacent to the ferry terminal, a minor league baseball park overlooked the harbor and the Big Apple. Near the left field fence, there stood a 9/11 memorial aimed at the Twin Towers. Until I saw Richmond County Ballpark, I thought PNC Park in Pittsburgh had the best view of any stadium.

Pat drove me through the borough, bringing back memories of my days at Wagner. We stopped at a handful of restaurants that were closed—strange for noon on a Friday. Then we headed for the Westerleigh Tennis Club. The three courts and tiny clubhouse are a gem that one can't imagine in a city of eight million people. Pat and I sat in rocking chairs on the porch and were entertained by a doubles match on the clay courts.

Then, after a short drive to Clove Lakes Park, we enjoyed a wonderful lunch at the Stone House on the lake. After the meal, we stopped off at Wagner College and watched the field hockey team practicing on the newly constructed Astroturf field. Wagner is a small liberal arts school with 2,200 students. Most of the facilities are shared. So, I felt her great pride when Pat said, "This is the first facility Wagner has built exclusively for women."

Pat and John at lunch at Cloves Lakes Park

After a brief ride through the St. John's University campus, we planned one more stop: her house. Driving down Park Lane brought back fifty-year-old memories of a time when I came of age. As I entered Pat's home, the first thing I noticed was the fireplace. Even though there was no fire burning, it brought back a very warm feeling. We chatted with her husband, George, for an hour or so. Then she drove me back to the ferry terminal for my return trip and another hug. As the boat cruised across the harbor, I reflected on a wonderful afternoon spent with a wonderful person.

The ferry docked at The Battery, and I followed the flock of commuters through the terminal. The herd led me to the great underground transportation system of New York City. I wandered through the concourse and eventually found my way to the W train entrance. Once again, I could have switched trains and boarded the express. But as I took my seat on the local, I savored my afternoon with Pat and resumed one of my favorite pastimes: people-watching. New York City is known as the melting pot, since so many cultures have settled into the city that never rests. With almost every person who entered the car, my mind made up a story. *Didn't I see that man's picture on the post office wall?*

As the train rumbled down the tracks, a million thoughts raced through my mind. But one stood out. *This seventy-four-year-old guy has come a long way. I wonder where I would have wound up had Pat not entered my life.*

JOHN ROCHE

John Roche grew up in Brooklyn, New York, and moved in 1974 to Pittsburgh, Pennsylvania, where he met and married a western Pennsylvania redhead. Forty-eight years later, they are still together.

John received a BS in economics from Wagner College, Staten Island, New York. During college, he drove a taxi in New York City. Many years later, he continued his education at California University of Pennsylvania by working toward a master's degree in homeland security. He dropped out halfway through the program; between working two jobs, raising a family, and trying to have a social life, he just burned out.

John served in the US Air Force Reserve and worked at the federal Office of Personnel Management until 2015. Between 1996 and 2014, he moonlighted as a chauffeur in Pittsburgh. Now retired, John spends his time writing his life stories, playing piano, cooking, golfing, and living his life as a half-master.

Heartbreak Moments

Lisa Marie Webb

"Hi, I'm looking for Mrs. Randle's room. Has she arrived yet? I'm her daughter."

"No. The medical transport should arrive shortly though."

"Oh, good. I'm glad I arrived first. I have some items for her room to make it a little more comfy. Is it okay if I take them in before she arrives?"

"Sure. Follow me. I'll show you where she'll be."

"Thank you." I turned to follow the nurse down the hall.

"No problem. Here's her room. If you need anything, I'll be back at the nurses' station."

I brought in the bags and busied myself checking the clothes, photos, toiletries, and such from Mom's condo. *Do I have everything? It's kind of bare in here. Maybe I can pick up a few things to add color.* I grabbed my cell phone to search for nearby stores but became lost in thought.

The hospital doctor's ominous words flitted through my memory like unwanted specters accompanied by the shrill shiver of nails on a chalkboard: "She did not bounce back after the emergency room rehydrated her. Yes, I'm sure . . . some type of dementia. It looks like Alzheimer's at this point . . . maybe mixed with vascular. We can't send her home. Someone will have to care for her. After rehab, I recommend you admit her to a locked facility. It will be too hard on your own in her condition."

The doctor kept me updated by phone as I prepared to travel to Ohio for an unknown amount of time.

Locked facility? No way. I was just here three weeks ago. She wasn't like this. How could this happen so quickly?

Eventually, the transport arrived, transferring Mom from the hospital to the rehabilitation center, and my thoughts wrenched back to the present. My heart churned at the first glimpse of her riding the raised, white-sheeted gurney as it rounded the elevator corner into the hall. *Alzheimer's? I don't understand. Maybe he's wrong.* Mom wore an eyes-wide expression on her face. I spoke to her, hoping my familiar voice would have a calming effect.

"Hi, Mom." The look in her eyes—a mix of *being lost* with a dash of *seeing beyond*—was like heartache on steroids to me. "Mom, it's me, Lisa Marie. I'm right here beside you."

The transport team rolled by me into Mom's room. Her eyes began to register the here and now as she tried to keep them pinned on me. The technicians prepared Mom to transfer to her assigned bed. She craned her neck to see around them, so I moved farther into the room to make it easier for her eye contact.

She looks small, incomplete somehow.

Clasps clicked and black nylon straps zipped as they were pulled through and left to hang gurney-side.

Mom bobbed and weaved to keep her view of me while the team moved around her and performed their tasks. A clinical, chemical smell wafted about the room as they worked.

"Okay, Mrs. Randle. We are going to help you. Are you ready?" They continued—though Mom did not respond to them, her pleading eyes still pinned on me. They lowered the gurney even with the bed. She held onto the shiny chrome side rails like a child perched on an amusement park ride until they lowered them.

"All right, Mrs. Randle, here we go. Can you slide over to the bed for me?" Once they completed their task, they quickly exited, leaving only Mom, her plastic hospital discharge bag of personal belongings, the rehab staff member, and me.

"Hi, Mom. Did you have an adventure riding on the gurney?"

No words. She just looked at me with an odd, questioning, helpless expression I'd never seen on her face.

Who is this? This is the right body, but this is not her. I looked at the nurse, feeling rather lost as to how to help Mom. *It's as if someone popped her open and scooped out her essence. Where is that fiercely independent, spunky, master's-degreed woman with the beautiful smile I've known all my life? Lord, help me. What do I do?*

"Mom, let's put your things away, okay?" After the faintest affirmation from her, I unpacked her things. I'd waited for her so she could see what I brought and where things would go. "Shall we put your toiletries in this bedside drawer, so you can reach them easily? What about the dresser? The drawers are pretty big. We can put your undies, socks, and nightclothes in the top drawer. I'll hang your clothes here in the wardrobe, okay?"

On I went, asking and doing, trying to involve and comfort her until everything was done. Mom sat, looking sheepish, as if she had no idea what was happening, but went along with whatever I was doing. The whole time I was there, she barely moved unless I prompted her. I stayed as long as I could, hoping it would help her settle in—and so I could deal with the staff coming in and out with all the necessary new patient information and questions, which were beyond what Mom could handle in her condition.

The rest of the time, I watched television with her, made conversation, and encouraged her to eat a little something. Eventually, it was time to go. Several errands required attention on her behalf, including going to her condo to search for legal information I needed to help her.

My sixty-seven-year-young mother watched as I prepared to go. With a kiss and a promise I'd be back soon, I headed toward the door. Mom promptly rose from the edge of the bed—where she'd sat most of the day with her hands in her lap—and followed me. At the door, I turned, hugged her, and kissed her again, hoping she'd stay.

"Mom, will you finish watching the TV show so you can tell me how it ends when I return?"

"Okay." She nodded but stuck to me like glue as I stepped into the hall.

"I have to go now. I'll be back, okay?" With a ripping wave of emotion, I turned away, stepped toward the elevator, and again asked her to watch how the show ended.

Her voice said, "Okay," but the look in her eyes was like a lasso squeezing my heart. I wanted to stay and comfort her, but I needed to leave. Heading down the corridor toward the elevator, I heard the most child-like voice come from her. "Can I go with you?"

Turning, I saw. There she stood, looking like a lost child in the hallway, with one pant leg at her ankle and the other calf-high, exposing the new security monitor they had strapped on her—as they would do to a prisoner—when she arrived. The scarf fell askew on her head with tendrils of brown curls peeking out. Cracks eked through my heart like fissures on the western seaboard near a soon-erupting fault.

"Where are you going?"

Bracing to get my words out without falling apart, I said, "I'm sorry, Mom. I have to get going." I felt my heart break at that moment. I hurried toward the elevator—it would not open if her ankle bracelet came too near.

"Can I go with you?" She moved as if to come toward me.

"No, sorry, you have to stay here." *I hate this.*

"Whyyyy?" Her voice sounded small and frail, nothing like the commanding, forceful sound I grew up hearing.

I looked back. I wished I hadn't.

She looked wounded and frightened, as if being abandoned. The image of my mother standing in the middle of the hall—looking forlorn and full of bewilderment—was emblazoned onto my mind. The sight crushed my heart.

"You're leaving me?"

As I pushed the down button, I put on my best face and used the most comforting voice I could muster. "Never. I have to run an errand. I'll come back." Then, grateful our cousin worked there, I added, "Carolyn will visit later."

"Take me with you?" It was almost a whimper.

"I can't. It's an appointment. I'll return. I promise." *Hold it together . . . hold it together.* Finally, the elevator doors opened. *Just breathe.*

With a wave, a forced smile, and a blown kiss, I stepped into the elevator, pushed the destination button, leaned against the back wall with all my energy drained, and lost it. I tasted the salt of rare, hot tears that slowly flowed down my face, each carrying shards of my heart.

God, I need your help.

The slow elevator descended with a hydraulic bump at the bottom. The floor number was announced in digital red. I wiped my face. The sluggish doors opened. I stepped through

Mom (Val) and Lisa Marie,
hanging out

Mom (Val) before Alzheimer's
disease

Mom (Val) still smiling, almost the end

Lisa Marie Webb

them as if into a new world. A world where I was now in charge of my mother. Her caregiver.

⅋

Almost eight years later. Rest in peace, Mom.
I did my best.
Thank you, Lord, for your help.

LISA MARIE WEBB

Lisa Marie Webb, originally from Ohio, now writes from the sunny state of Florida after twenty-four years of military service and several years as a caregiver for her mother. Lisa Marie's literary work centers around memoir, fiction, and inspirational nonfiction. She also enjoys travel, music, and photography. Currently, Lisa Marie is learning the art of fly fishing, fly tying, and rod building with other veterans. One day, she plans to have a strong, beautiful black dog named Apollo.

CarFaces

Steven Weisberg

The television studio floor manager arched his right hand, tightening it into a fist above his head as fanfare played from the band. Pointing his index finger like the barrel of a revolver, he pistol-whipped it downward in the direction of talent for the cue.

"Hi, I'm Joey Bishop, son of a gun, and I'm Mike's co-host!"

Neon-white applause signs flashed off-camera as Mike Douglas bounced from behind a groovy-colored, starburst-patterned stage curtain, beaming his signature crooner's smile. With the smooth verve of a seasoned performer, he belted out the opening number, setting a good-time mood for today's *Mike Douglas Show*. From the studios of KYW-TV in Philadelphia, it was lighthearted daytime talk show entertainment for thoroughly bored and mostly isolated house-wives across the nation.

On this particular day of April 20, 1977, I had been stra-tegically planted in a third-row aisle seat, right of center stage, where I focused on the floor manager for what would be *my* cue for talent. At twenty-six, I was just out of graduate school, flat broke, and underemployed. But I had an original idea that I thought might play funny on TV.

Twenty minutes into the show—after the Preservation Hall Jazz Band performed a Dixieland medley and Mabel King recounted stories about her role in the Broadway version of *The Wiz* and Corbett Monica reminisced about doing an opening act for Rat Pack members Frank Sinatra, Sammy Davis Jr., and Dean Martin—Joey turned to Mike.

"What's next?"

Mike, right on cue, replied enthusiastically, "Let's discover new talent—right after this break."

As stage lights dimmed, the floor manager checked his clipboard for the show rundown and pointed directly at me. Nodding back, I stretched my arms outward and pondered the moment. *This will be my first-ever TV appearance.* I felt surprisingly calm, ruminating on words of wisdom from my mom. "No matter what happens," she said, "go . . . and have a good time."

To a round of applause, the stage lights came back up with cameras focused on Joey standing in the audience. "Let's discover new talent! Who's first?"

A hand shot up in front of him.

"Right over here," Joey said, instructing the camera crew to follow.

He lowered the microphone to a middle-aged man, smartly tailored in a three-piece suit, seated across the aisle to my left. His salt-and-pepper hair, combed into a pompadour, complemented his thick-lensed tortoiseshell glasses.

"And what's your talent?" Joey asked.

"I'm going to perform 'Hava Nagila' . . . on my fist!"

It elicited an uncertain grimace from Joey as the man stood and curled his left hand into a tightened ball. His forefinger and thumb formed a fleshy mouthpiece onto which he pressed and buzzed his lips. Ingeniously, constricting and releasing tension in his fisted hand mimicked the sound of a ram's horn.

Joe Harnell and the Band, Mike's backup group, picked up the frantic, kazoo-like klezmer tempo, inspiring the busload of ladies from the old-age home to clap in syncopated rhythm. Fist-Man's performance ended on a *tekiah gedolah*, the last blast of the shofar concluding Jewish High Holiday services, and to a musical flourish from the band, the audience applauded wildly—with one exception. The woman seated directly in front of Fist-Man was noticeably irate, wiping herself dry after being serenaded in a hurricane of spit.

"Who's next?" Joey asked.

The floor manager snapped his fingers in my direction. I bolted upright.

"Oh, isn't it good they put them so close together?" Joey quipped, pointing the microphone at me. "And what's your name?"

"Steven Weisberg."

"Steven Weisberg?" Joey paused. "Of the Jewish faith?"

With a Harpo Marx–like grin, I raised my eyebrows impishly and murmured, "Uh-huh!"

"Take all . . . the time . . . you want!"

I waved to Mike off-camera, fidgeting with his fingers as if he'd lost control of the show. Joey had just bestowed full permission for me to act up and act out, and now, as one of the *chosen people* who had been chosen to perform, I drew from the mercurial cauldron of bad behavior in Hebrew school that had generated innumerable detentions.

"Where ya from?" Joey continued in his native Philadelphia accent.

"South Philadelphia . . . Sixth and Wolf," I proudly asserted, knowing full well Joseph Gottlieb, aka Joey Bishop, hailed from the same neighborhood at Third and Snyder.

"Sixth and Wolf . . . ? Joey beamed exuberantly, then, rummaging through the fog of memory, inquired, "By the park?"

"We lived right across the street," I replied with unbridled chutzpah, even though, in reality, it was my maternal grandparents who lived there until 1960. Still, when South Philadelphia Jewish boys get together, an unspoken code exists between them.

"Very good," Joey said.

I feel I've just been initiated into the Rat Pack.

"And . . . what's your talent?"

"I do facial impressions of classic automobiles."

Joey pointed toward the stage and deadpanned, "I'll get you for this one, Mike."

Then, turning to the musical fist, Joey murmured, "Stay close. You might be on again."

Up to this point, my only solo stage appearance consisted of my bar mitzvah haftarah. I learned it by listening to a box set of 45 rpm records featuring synagogue cantor Sidney Karpo. At thirteen, I became a man thanks to a karaoke version of "Sing Along with Sidney."

I never perceived myself as cute, adorable, or remotely attractive. However, I majored in theater at college and knew I could play that character by acting affably upbeat, offbeat, and playfully off-the-wall, like Soupy Sales on TV. In fact, in homage to Mr. Sales, I dressed in a black-and-multi-colored sweater over a button-down shirt, like the sweater outfit he wore on *Lunch with Soupy Sales,* his inspirational Saturday-morning television show.

Listening to Mom tell funny stories when I was a kid, I absorbed her craft for comedic timing, observation, reflection, and projection. Courtesy of television, I studied the masters: Lenny Bruce, George Carlin, Jonathan Winters, David

Brenner, and Robert Klein. Now, given the power of the close-up on TV, this would be my time to try out an original visually oriented comedy routine.

The premise was pure Hebrew school, gleaned from Genesis.

"You see, Joey, when God created man, he created him in his own image. But when man got to the point he, too, could create, he created his master invention, the automobile, in his likeness too. Hoods looked like noses; headlights were eyes; grills . . . lips and teeth."

Holding a full-page magazine ad beside my head, I continued. "Take, for example, the 1955 Chevy. It predated Jimmy Carter's presidential smile."

Mimicking the picture of the car, I cocked my head to a side, stretched my lips to show all my upper and lower teeth, and re-created the exaggerated toothy grin of the then-popular president.

Some people laughed. Joey Bishop chimed in, "Yeah, I see it. He does look like that."

Holding up a picture of the next car, I explained, "The 1952 Buick looked like Lon Chaney in *The Phantom of the Opera* . . . just when the girl takes off his mask."

Steven impersonating the Citroën while Joey Bishop looks on

I jutted out my jaw, bulged my eyes as wide open as I could, and bared my lower teeth like a shark about to attack.

It got a bigger laugh, and I continued with more cockamamie observations and contorted facial impressions.

"The 1949 Studebaker looked like Alfred Hitchcock puckering up for a kiss."

"The Citroën from France looked confused because they put the steering wheel on the *right* side of the car."

With each facial impression, the laughs grew louder. I could tell the routine was connecting in an off-kilter but intelligent way: visually funny with pop-culture references and satire based in scripture.

"And finally, the 1957 Edsel looked like Henry Ford biting into a lemon!" For this impression, I crossed my eyes to resemble twin headlights, sucked my lips together, and pushed them upward while scrunching my nose. It was the most excruciating face to make and the most exaggerated one in my repertoire. I held the pose for as long as I could physically endure it. The band played fanfare ending the bit, nearly drowning out the applause.

"Very good, Steve. You're funny," Joey said on camera. "You're going to be a comedian. I tell you this because you have a comedy mind." Then, pointing to Fist-Man, Joey added, "And he can be your orchestra."

I left the studio that day having had not just a good time but the time of my young life.

What transpired next came at me faster than I could possibly have imagined or was ready to handle: articles in the Associated Press, *TV Guide*, and *US* magazine; appearances on NBC's *Tomorrow with Tom Snyder* and being seen on *Saturday Night Live*.

"Very good, Steve. You're funny." Joey's words resonated and haunted me as I knew I could never duplicate or ever approximate that incredible, meteoric success. Ever since, I've relentlessly tried to prove time and again that my "comedy mind," as Joey called it, was truly authentic and my initial success was not the sheer luck of an imposter.

STEVEN WEISBERG

Philadelphia-born Steven Weisberg is a post-war baby boomer, a survivor of the Philadelphia Public School system, and a member of Gen TV. He followed early instincts and his family's adoration for the performing arts to pursue a career in radio and television as a writer, editor, and producer at NBC, CBS, FOX, and PBS. Now retired in South Florida, Steven writes life stories and memoirs with a *Mad Magazine* skew.

It's Not About the Money

Orah Zamir

I lived on the Upper West Side of New York City for ten years, at Seventy-First Street and Broadway. Being in the center of music and a variety of Jewish experiences gave me an exciting life. I could walk to work at the Metropolitan Opera Guild. My apartment was small but tall and comfortable. It was filled with books, music, and Judaica.

One night, I arrived home and came upon a commotion at the front door of my building. A bag lady carrying two large shopping bags was sitting so that she blocked the front door. She appeared to be short and thin. She wore layers of blue and white that looked like a rag, and a hat with a brim sat lopsided on her head. Someone had called the police, and we awaited their arrival.

Then a man-and-woman team arrived wearing police uniforms and carrying guns and sticks. The man, who obviously didn't want to touch the dirty woman, held out his stick and gestured for her to get up. She reached up, clutched at the stick, pulled herself up, grabbed her bags, and scurried off.

The policewoman asked some questions of the residents and then said, "She might want to go to a shelter for the night. I'm going to go after her." She rushed away.

Nobody moved.

The policewoman returned, looking confused. "She did not want to go to a shelter. Those shopping bags she was carrying were filled with money."

This incident had a deep effect on me because I had thought poverty was about money. If it was not about the money, what was it about? Why did I have trouble supporting myself? I worked but could not earn enough money to meet my basic needs. I would pay parts of utility bills just to keep going. I was in survival mode.

I became a work addict—always looking at the want ads, always either working, looking for work, or feeling guilty about not working. I beat myself up because there was never enough. I thought, *If only I could earn more money, everything would be great.* I had visions of becoming a bag lady—until I met one.

Years earlier, when I moved to New York, I had fallen in love with Yiddish music. I decided to learn the language by attending the Summer Program in Yiddish Language and Culture sponsored by *Yidisher Visnshaftlekher Institut* (YIVO Institute for Jewish Research), a Yiddish organization that has an extensive archive of materials related to Eastern European Jewish culture and immigration. My first week in the class, I made a friend, Jill, who was a student in the Department of Performance Studies at NYU. Jill was working toward a PhD in dance. The department focused on the essence of what creates magic in any kind of performance, whether it is in the theater, the street, or a house of worship. They hired a respected Jewish anthropologist to head the department. She came to speak to us. Jill introduced me to her, and the next thing I knew, I was a graduate student at NYU.

I had a partial scholarship for tuition and a work-study job in the department that paid my daily expenses. I lived on loans the five years I was a student. When I lost my job in the department, I went to the work-study office where three-by-five-inch cards lined the walls with open jobs. Not one of them appealed to me—quite a change from my days of haunting want ads. On a whim, I went to the library and applied for a job there.

The woman looked at my application, smiled at me, and said, "Have I got a job for you."

The job was inputting music records into the Library of Congress system. It was perfect. I loved it. I could listen to music on a Walkman while I worked. I made friends with the staff. I did so well, my supervisors decided to train me to catalog music. They upgraded me from work-study to employee and gave me a raise.

During my years at NYU, my life took a turn that was to teach me what life was really all about. I learned that the year I moved to New York, the first woman cantor graduated from a Jewish seminary. (A cantor carries the Jewish musical tradition and leads prayers in the synagogue.) Then, Debbie Katchko founded the Women Cantors' Network. Thinking back to high school, I recognized that I received life from participation in the synagogue. I was a leader in the youth group. I sang in the choir, although at that time, I had nowhere to go on that path. Women as cantors were not even a dream yet.

Things had changed.

I attended the first meeting of the WCN as a journalist. There, I met women who were studying at a college in Philadelphia and becoming cantors. I graduated from NYU in February 1985, moved in August, and started school in September.

My mother passed away in October. I was in New York at the time, staying with a friend. My brother, fortunately, had her phone number and called to tell me. Instead of returning to Philadelphia, I went to Boston for the funeral. It was a painful experience.

The extended family jibed at me for not appreciating my mother. They did not know the narcissistic side of her that projected *her* issues onto me and made *me* the problem. When the casket was brought into the chapel, it hit me: *That is my mother's body.*

What I did not know until I returned to Philadelphia was, I had taken on energy from her. In this life energy, both during life and in death, remained a legacy of family and Jewish trauma that led me into years of internal struggle and of discovering that my poverty was, indeed, not about the money. It was about restoring the soul this trauma had stolen from me.

When I returned from the funeral, I started life in Philadelphia. I attended school and needed work. My supervisor at NYU knew that Temple University Library was holding 2,500 pieces of music in a literal cage because no one there could catalog them. That became my job. When the music was all on the shelves for the benefits of education and joy, I moved on.

I taught Hebrew school and music, and I tutored bar and bat mitzvah students. I also conducted life cycle ceremonies such as bar and bat mitzvahs, weddings, funerals, and baby naming ceremonies. Although circumcision for boys was as old as the Jewish religion, there had been no communal welcoming for girls until recently. I loved those ceremonies. I was learning the values of my heritage, growing spiritually, and discovering true abundance.

While studying and working, I tried to deal with my personal issues. Money was the most immediate, so I went to a program to help with financial issues. In a meeting, someone said, "It's not about the money." That reminded me of the bag lady who had taught me that lesson from experience several years before. As I worked the program, I learned true abundance was in growing spiritually, finding purpose, and doing what I loved.

Life was normal for three years. In the last year, however, I was diagnosed with breast cancer. After a year of surgery, radiation, and chemotherapy, I finished school and graduated. My student job ended.

I tried to audition for cantorial positions, but I did not have the strength. One day, I got a phone call from a cantor I had met at a retreat. She said, "How would you like to go to Bermuda?"

At the same time, I went on welfare and went cruising on a five-star ship to Bermuda for a week to conduct Jewish High Holiday worship. It was perfect. I discovered I loved the sea. I conducted a few short services for which I had written an original High Holiday prayer book. I rested on the days we were at sea and fell in love with *moon gates* in Bermuda.

My soul, which had been lost in childhood, was opening up and beginning to express itself, although I would not learn the underlying core issue, childhood trauma, and truly begin to heal until much later. An era was over, but a new one was about to begin. I was being guided by something beyond myself as the search for my soul took another new turn: It would be about abundance, but not money. My spirit guides were arranging for my needs to be met as I worked on my healing process and my spiritual purpose.

ORAH ZAMIR

Orah Zamir, a retired chaplain and spiritual guide, has been writing since her school years. One of the papers she wrote for her AP English class was pronounced by her teacher as "the best piece of student writing I've seen" and was published in the school literary magazine.

Orah earned a BS in journalism from the University of Illinois, an MA from NYU (her thesis was published on https://www.westsideminyan .org/), and an MA from Gratz College in Philadelphia.

Orah is a survivor of childhood trauma. She is currently writing a memoir describing her life's journey and the healing process she went through. Orah lives in Philadelphia, Pennsylvania, with her cat, Angel. She is interested in spirituality and meditation, and she enjoys coloring mandalas. The new *Divine Feminine* and the cultural evolution of our times are of special interest to her. Read more of Orah's work on her blog: medium.com/@journeywoman15.

PATRICIA CHARPENTIER, author of the multi-award-winning book, *Eating an Elephant: Write Your Life One Bite at a Time*, teaches, writes, edits, ghostwrites, and publishes personal and family history and life-based stories. To date, Patricia has coauthored, edited, and published more than seventy personal and family histories. Her belief about capturing life stories is: The only way to do this wrong is to not do it at all.

Patricia founded the Life Writers membership in 2020. Life Writers combines three components, which she believes are necessary for success—community, instruction, and accountability—and brings people together online from across the US, Canada, Mexico, and Jamaica. Learn more at LifeWriters.us.

To encourage writing in community, Patricia offers free, virtual First Tuesday Write and Read sessions every month where people from across the globe come together to write in response to prompts and share their writing in small groups.

Visit Patricia at WritingYourLife.org and LifeWriters.us.

CPSIA information can be obtained
at www.ICGtesting.com
Printed in the USA
LVHW081907130123
737140LV00005B/68

9 781939 472403